AUSTRALIAN HOMESCHOOLING SERIES

T0363254

Successful English 8B

Years 8–10

CORONEOS PUBLICATIONS

Item No 563

This book is available from recognised booksellers or contact:

Coroneos Publications

Telephone: (02) 9838 9265   **Facsimile:** (02) 9838 8982
Business Address: 2/195 Prospect Highway Seven Hills 2147
Website: www.coroneos.com.au
E-mail: info@fivesenseseducation.com.au

Item # 563
Successful English 8B
by Valerie Marett
First published 2017

ISBN: 978-1-922034-72-4
© Valerie Marett

Contents

Using the Best Word

While it is useful to know words that are more or less synonymous, we must be careful how we use them in sentences because the English language has thousands of words that are in some degree synonymous, but very few are so fully synonymous as to be interchangeable on every occasion.

Only one of the synonyms given in brackets can be correctly used in each sentence. Insert the correct word in the space provided. Use your dictionary to help you.

1. It was unreasonable to expect a _____ old lady to stand up to such a strenuous programme. (fragile, frail, brittle)

2. Outside his window he heard the ugly _____ of a crowd demanding revenge. (din, clamour, tumult, uproar)

3. Even his speech had an _____ flavour, suggesting he had lived long in close association with the soil. (earthy, earthy, terrestrial)

4. A superstitious person will regard the appearance of a black cat as a good _____. (prognostication, prophecy, omen)

5. A hot, humid day makes one feel _____. (apathetic, lethargic, slothful)

6. Above the _____ of gigantic waves crashing against the rocks he could just hear the ship's siren. (clamour, tumult, uproar)

7. The great rock was _____ asunder as the pressure increased. (cleaved, divided)

8. The tropics are said to have an _____ climate because of the extremes of rainfall and temperature. (immoderate, unbridled, violent, intemperate, excessive, inordinate)

9. Astrology is a/an _____ science. (hidden, occult, concealed)

10. The Poet Laureate is expected to write _____ verses to mark great national events. (irregular, occasional, intermittent)

Subordinate Clause

A subordinate clause adds meaning to a principal clause.

    e.g., When the rain ceased we hurried home.
we hurried home—principal clause
When the rain ceased— subordinate clause.

Common subordinate conjunctions are: after, although, as, because, even if, even though, if, provided, rather than, since, so that, than, though, unless, until, whether, which, when, why.

A.   **Find the principal and the subordinate clause in each sentence and write them in the lines provided.**

1.   When painting, Margaret hummed a song to herself.

   Principal clause: _____

   Subordinate clause: _____

2.   John takes his time when reading a menu.

   Principal clause: _____

   Subordinate clause: _____

3.   Because our office throws away so much paper we should start a recycling programme.

   Principal clause: _____

   Subordinate clause: _____

4.   We stayed in the garden with Dad since Mum was washing the floors.

   Principal clause: _____

   Subordinate clause: _____

5.   Susan has a mobile phone that she talks on all the time.

   Principal clause: _____

   Subordinate clause: _____

6.   He hit a ball directly at me which I caught.

   Principal clause: _____

   Subordinate clause: _____

7.   Mary ate the swordfish at the restaurant although she hated it.

   Principal clause: _____

   Subordinate clause: _____

Adjectival Clause

An adjectival clause is a subordinate clause which adds meaning to a noun. It does the work of an adjective.

> e.g., A man who has plenty of money should give generously.
> A man should give generously (main clause)
> (A man who) has plenty of money (subordinate clause)
> The subordinate clause refers to the man so it is adjectival.

Underline the adjectival clause in each of the following sentences. Circle the noun it modifies or relates to.

1. Mike, whose ancestors came from Ireland, marched in the St Patrick's Day Parade.

2. Maths, which is David's favourite subject, has always been easy for him.

3. There is the house that I'd like to buy.

4. We live an hour from Tullamarine, which is Victoria's largest airport.

5. Is that the jacket you want to buy?

6. Caulfield is the town where your father was born.

7. Mr Harman is a history teacher who also coaches basketball.

8. Is this the letter you were expecting?

9. Across the road is the school that I attended.

10. For dinner we had fried chicken which is my favourite dish.

Adjectival Phrase

Adjectival phrases add meaning to or describe nouns or pronouns. They may begin with a preposition or present or past participle.

> e.g., The boy <u>near me</u> was reading a book. (near me—adjectival phrases)

Underline the adjectival phrase in each of the following sentences. Circle the noun it modifies or relates to.

1. I saw a rare elephant with a white skin.

2. My grandfather is a man of great wisdom.

3. The price of the boots was too high.

France & England—The Struggle for Power

Between 1688 and 1815 the two main powers were France and England. During this time both Britain and France were trying to expand their trade routes and establish Empires to purchase their products as well as supply new ones.

There were several general causes for the hostility between the two countries. Firstly, Louis XIV was trying to extend the boundaries of France to the River Rhine. This could only be done at the expense of the German States in the South East, and of the Netherlands, (now Belgium and Holland) in the North East. Spain owned half of the Netherlands and the other half was independent. Since there was no natural boundary between the Spanish Netherlands and France, a line of "Barrier Fortresses" had been erected. France was slowly gaining control of these, and once she had total control, she could seize Holland as well.

Secondly, at various times between 1688 and 1815, France's rulers attempted to control the policy of Spain by means of a close family alliance or a treaty. Also Louis XIV (1643-1715), at the beginning of this period and the French Revolution and Napoleon (1793-1815) at the end of the period, had achieved a position in Europe which threatened the independence of all other countries.

The cause of this constant warfare between England and France was not solely European. There was commercial and colonial rivalry between the two countries and their ambitions clashed throughout the world. In India, in the West Indies, and in North America, a great struggle took place which was really a struggle for trade and Empire.

In the War of English Succession, over who should rule on the English throne, France supported James II against William. It was important to Louis that William should be defeated for an alliance between William and Holland meant Louis would not gain his ambition and over-run the Netherlands. William, won and his life work was to defend Holland against Louis using England's economic and naval power. By 1697 England had gained supremacy on the sea and in a peace treaty Louis had to recognise William as King of England.

Peace didn't last very long as the question of a successor to the Spanish throne arose. This affected all of Europe as the Spanish dominions included not only Spain and the Netherlands but also Naples, Sicily, Sardinia as well as vast possessions in the West Indies and South America.

A war to decide this lasted from 1702-1713. England entered the war to check the power of France, which would be overwhelming if France gained control of Spain; to safeguard English trade, which was threatened by Louis and to prevent a restoration of the Stuart kings.

English victories on the continent of Europe and at sea resulted in colonial gains in the Treaty of Utrecht in 1713 when England gained from France the Hudson Bay Territory, Nova Scotia and Newfoundland. From Spain she gained Gibraltar and Minorca and Spain also granted Britain monopoly in supplying trade to the Spanish colonies.

A. **Read the comprehension on the opposite page and then answer the questions in sentences.**

1. Who were the main powers in the struggle?

   _____

2. Briefly list the causes of hostility between these two countries.

   _____

   _____

   _____

   _____

3. Why did it matter to Louis XIV who ruled on the English throne?

   _____

   _____

4. What important event had occurred by 1697?

   _____

5. Explain how the question of a successor to the Spanish throneaffected all of Europe.

   _____

   _____

6. Britain waged a war to decide this from 1702-1713. What were her reasons for the war?

   _____

   _____

7. Think! Why is learning about the period in history between 1688 and 1815 important to us in Australia?

   _____

   _____

B. Vocabulary: Find a word in the text that meets the following definitions.

1. the right or act by which one person comes
   next in the line to rule   _____

2. a group of people who leave their native country
   to form a settlement in a new land, ruled by or
   connected to the parent state.   _____

Australian Poetry Through the Ages: Convict Ballads

Bush songs or bush ballads are a poetry tradition in Australian outback, which may be said or sung. The rhyming songs, poems and tales often speak of the convict beginning and the itinerant and rebellious spirit of Australia as a young country.

The songs and poems tell personal stories of life in the wide open country of Australia. Typical subjects include mining, raising and droving cattle, sheep shearing, war stories, the Shearers Strike of 1891, conflicts between the landless working class and the squatters and outlaws such as Ned Kelly.
There were also numerous sea shanties sung by whalers and other sailors. as well as songs about the voyage made by convicts and other immigrants from England to Australia.

Here are two of the most popular convict ballads. The authors of both are not known. Read them carefully and think about them.

The Girl with the Black Velvet Band

It was in the city of London
In apprenticeship I was bound
And many's the gay old hour
I spent in that dear old town

Chorus:
And her eyes they shone like diamonds
I thought her the pride of the land
The hair that hung down on her shoulder
Was tied with a black velvet band

One day as I was walking
Along my usual beat
A pretty little young maiden
Came tripping along the street

Chorus:

One day as we were a walking
A gentleman passed us by
I could see she was bent on some mischief
By the rolling of her dark blue eye.

Chorus:

Gold watch she picked from his pocket
And slyly placed into my hand
I was taken in charge by a copper
Bad luck to that black velvet band

Chorus:

Before the Lord Mayor I was taken
Your case, sir, I plainly can see

© Valerie Marett
Coroneos Publications

Australian Homeschooling #563
Successful English 8B

And if I'm not greatly mistaken
You're bound far over the sea

Chorus:

It's over the dark and blue ocean
Far away to Van Diemen's Land
Away from my friends and relations
And the girl with the black velvet band

Chorus:

Old Botany Bay

Farewell to Old England forever
Farewell to my old pals as well
Farewell to the well known Old Bailee
Where I once used to be such a swell

Chorus:

Singing too-rall, li-oo-rall, li-ad-di-ty,
Singing too-rall, li-oo-rall, li-ay,
Singing too-rall, li-oo-rall, li-ad-di-ty
Oh we are bound for Botany Bay.

There's the captain as is our commandeer,
There's bo'sun and all the ship's crew
There's first and the second class passengers,
Knows what we poor convicts goes through.

Chorus:

'Taint leaving Old England we cares about,
'Taint 'cos we mispells wot we knows
But becos all we light finger'd gentry
Hop's around with a log on our toes.

Chorus:

Oh had I the wings of a turtle-dove,
I'd soar on my pinions so high,
Slap bang to the arms of my Polly love,
And in her sweet presence I'd die.

Chorus:

Now all my young Dookies and Duchesses,
Take warning from what I've to say,
Mind all is your own as you touch-es-es,
Or you'll find us in Botany Bay.

Answer these questions:

1. What rhyming pattern occurs in both poems?

_____

2. What effect do the short lines and the rhyming have on the ballads?

_____

_____

3. Both poems have choruses. How might this aid the appeal of the ballads?

_____

_____

4. Give 3 reasons why you think these ballads were so popular.

_____

_____

_____

_____

_____

5. What is the difference between a ballad and a poem?

_____

_____

6. Explain the meaning of the following terms:

a.   "log on our toes" _____

b.   "pinions"   _____

c.   "Old Bailee"   _____

7. Explain why the language used in the first ballad is different to the language in the second ballad.

_____

_____

8. The ballad refers to Van Diemen's Land. What is it called today?

_____

9. In what state is Botany Bay?

_____

Correct Usage

A. A verb agrees with its subject in person and number. Rewrite the sentences below choosing the correct verb from those in the brackets.

1. To every argument there (are, is) at least two sides.

   _____

2. None of them (seem, seems) to have made up his mind.

   _____

3. A party with a dog team (were, was) approaching the post.

   _____

4. Six weeks' leave per year (have, has) been granted to all workers.

   _____

5. Each man and woman in the group (were carrying, was carrying) a heavy load.

   _____

B. Correct the sentences below by replacing the wrong words in each sentence with the correct word or words in the list under the sentence.

1. The teacher read "Treasure Island" to him and I.
   a. he   b. me   c. them

   _____

2. To Jane and I the news came as a complete surprise.
   a. me   b. both Jayne and I   c. to me and Jayne   d. for

   _____

3. But I am not the person you are searching for.
   a. which   b. whom   c. for whom   d. for that

   _____

4. Who do you think committed the robbery?
   a. did   b. who   c. don't you   d. has committed

   _____

5. Paul said him and me were the best players on the team.
   a. better   b. me and him   c. he and I   d. he

   _____

© Valerie Marett
Coroneos Publications

Australian Homeschooling #563
Successful English 8B

Adjectival Phrase or Adjectival Clause

An adjectival phrase adds meaning to or describes nouns or pronouns. It may begin with a preposition or present or past participle.

e.g., The boy <u>near me</u> was reading a book. (near me—adjectival phrases)

The airplane, waiting at the end of the runway, is the next to take off. (waiting at the end of the runway—adjectival phrase with a present participle.)

An adjectival clause is a subordinate clause which adds meaning to a noun. It does the work of an adjective.

e.g., A man who has plenty of money should give generously.
A man should give generously (main clause)
(A man) has plenty of money (subordinate clause)
The subordinate clause refers to the man so it is adjectival.

A.   Identify the adjectival phrase in each sentence. Underline it.

1.   The name of that city is Gawler.

2.   They are a couple without any children.

3.   The crowd, near the door, caused the delay.

4.   Everyone on the deck watched as the cruise ship pulled away from the wharf.

5.   Tom is a man with good instincts and a great sense of humour.

6.   While walking the dog, Mary hurt her leg.

B. Identify the adjectival clause in each sentence. Underline it.

1.   Is that the cake that you brought?

2.   Here is the jacket you asked for.

3.   Billy is the friend who helped me.

4.   Maths, which is Peter's favourite subject, has always been easy for him.

5.   Is that the jacket you'd like to buy?

6.   The dog, that you found roaming, belongs to the Lawson's.

7.   For dinner we had roast chicken, which is my favourite meal.

Each sentence below contains either an adjectival clause or an adjectival phrase. Underline the adjectival phrase or adjectival clause. In the space provided state whether it is an adjectival clause or adjectival phrase.

1. Politicians who follow the party line generally do well.
   _____

2. The burglar, hearing a step, slipped behind the curtain.
   _____

3. His excuses, which were not convincing, angered his mother.
   _____

4. When the storm was over they went on with their game.
   _____

5. She is an author whom you will not have read.
   _____

6. Peter was made captain of the team because of his fine record.
   _____

7. During her final year of university Loraine discovered what it was to fall in love.
   _____

8. Cars that have diesel engines are still very popular.
   _____

9. The route that you recommended was not easy to follow.
   _____

10. Sonja was the daughter of a Norwegian immigrant.
   _____

11. The waitress with the pleasant smile served us today.
   _____

12. Did you see the man who was asking for you?
   _____

13. The couple with three children were among the first to board.
   _____

French and English in America

For twenty-six years after the signing of the Treaty of Utrecht peace was maintained between Britain and France. However trade relations between Britain and Spain became acute. The Spanish, although trying to jealously exclude other nations, were trading with their enormous trade possessions in South America, but did not develop the trade further.

British ships carried on a fair amount of illicit trade in South America. One British ship was allowed to trade annually. This ship emptied its cargo by day and then refilled its holds from small ships outside the harbour. This allowed them to continuously unload. The Spanish, incensed, tried to search English ships and often treated the British sailors harshly which aroused British feeling in England.

Finally in 1739 the War of Jenkin's Ear broke out. This was a trade war between England and Spain. Within a year this became part of a much larger struggle, the War of the Austrian Succession, (1740-48) and from 1744 hostilities between Britain and France were extended to North America and India. A seven year peace treaty between 1748 and 1756 really solved nothing.

From the time Samuel de Champlain founded New France in 1608, the French colony became caught in a colonial tug-of-war between England and France. Fighting was quick to erupt in North America, just like in Europe. But before the decisive battles, lands were constantly changing hands in smaller skirmishes. And as they went back and forth, place names often changed from French to English, and vice versa.

Britain had thirteen colonies along the North Atlantic seaboard in North America while the French held Louisiana, the Mississippi Basin and the estuary of the St. Lawrence River with trading posts at Quebec and Montreal. The French aimed to extend their forts and encircle the English by occupying the Ohio Basin. The English claimed that their colonies extended westward indefinitely so they sort to hold the Ohio basin. So an "unofficial war" started in 1748 and extended throughout the seven year peace.

The French started building a long line of fortresses to form a link between their northern and southern possessions and to hem in the British. The British, partly because of the disunity between the British Colonies, which did not allow for joint action, and partly because of delay from the Home Government in Britain, did little. The British Government did, however, grant large areas of the Valley for settlement, while the French replied by sending troops from Canada to warn off the British settlers.

In 1754 the French built Fort Duquesne near the western boundary of Pennsylvania on the Ohio and at the junction of three rivers. This led to immediate war. Two attempts to capture Fort Duquesne were made: the first under Washington in 1754 and the second under a British General, Braddock. Both were disastrous. The Red Indians, urged on by the French, made fierce attacks on the British colonists. It appeared likely the French would win when war was declared between Britain and France in 1756.

© Valerie Marett
Coroneos Publications

Australian Homeschooling #563
Successful English 8B

A. Answer these questions:

1. Where did Spain have trading interests?

   _____

2. Describe the way the British circumvented the Spanish permission allowing only one ship trade in South America each year.

   _____

   _____

   _____

3. In North America what two countries were rivals? What were they seeking?

   _____

   _____

4. What did the French try and do to ring in the British? What was the final result of this action?

   _____

   _____

   _____

5. Why do you think the French built Fort Duquesne near the junction of three rivers?

   _____

   _____

B. Word Knowledge: choose a word from the text that means the same as each word below.

1. a fight between two bodies of soldiers   _____

2. intense, sharp in effect   _____

3. enraged, very angry   _____

4. highly unsuccessful   _____

C. Research the War of Jenkins' Ear. Write a report. Include:

a. who the conflict was between

b. why it was named the War of Jenkins' Ear

c. why the conflict was notable

Australian Poetry Through the Ages: Bushrangers

Sometimes convicts escaped into the bush and became bushrangers. Bushrangers have always appealed to Australians although in truth they were robbers and murderers and there was little that was heroic about them

The ballads below are songs about two of Australia's well-known bushrangers, Jack Doolan and Ben Hall. Jack Doolan stabbed an apprentice and was sentenced to jail. When he came out he had a brief career as a bushranger. Ben Hall and his companions roamed an area of NSW from Bathurst to Forbes, south to Gundagai and east to Goulburn.

Here are two of the most popular bushranger ballads. The authors of both are not known. Read them carefully and think about them.

The Wild Colonial Boy

There was a wild colonial boy Jack Doolan was his name,
Of poor but honest parents he was born in Castlemaine.
He was his father's only hope, his mother's pride and joy,
And dearly did the parents love the wild colonial boy

Chorus:
Then, come all my hearties, we'll range the mountain side;
Together we will plunder, together we will ride.
We'll scour along the valleys and gallop o'er the plains,
We scorn to live in slavery bowed down with iron chains.

In 'sixty-one this daring youth commenced his wild career;
With a heart that knew no danger, no foeman did he fear;
He stuck up the Beechworth mailcoach and robbed Judge MacEvoy,
Who trembled and gave up his gold to the wild colonial boy.

Chorus

He bade the judge good morning, and told him to beware,
That he'd never rob a hearty chap who acted on the square;
And never to rob a mother of her son and only joy,
Or else you may turn outlaw like the wild colonial boy.

Chorus

One day as he was riding the mountain side along,
A-listening to the little birds, their pleasant laughing song
Three mounted troopers came in view, Kelly, Davis, and Fitzroy.
They thought that they would capture him, the wild colonial boy.

Chorus

Surrender now, Jack Doolan, you see there's three to one,
Surrender now, Jack Doolan, you daring highwayman!'

Jack drew a pistol from his belt and spun it like a toy,
'I'll fight but I won't surrender', cried the wild colonial boy.

Chorus

He fired at Trooper Kelly and brought him to the ground,
And in return from Davis received a mortal wound.
All shattered through the jaws he lay still firing at Fitzroy,
And that's the way they captured him, the wild colonial boy.

Chorus

Ballad of Ben Hall's Gang

Come all ye wild colonials
And listen to my tale;
A story of bushrangers' deeds
I will to you unveil.
'Tis of those gallant heroes,
Game fighters one and all;
And we'll sit and sing,
Long Live the King,
Dunn, Gilbert, and Ben Hall.

Ben Hall he was a squatter bloke
Who owned a thousand head;
A peaceful man he was until
Arrested by Sir Fred.
His home burned down, his wife cleared out,
His cattle perished all;
"They'll not take me a second time,"
Says valiant Ben Hall.

John Gilbert was a flash cove,
And John O'Meally too;
With Ben and Bourke and Johnny Vane
They all were comrades true.
They rode into Canowindra
And gave a public ball.
'Roll up, roll up, and have a spree,'
Says Gilbert and Ben Hall.

They took possession of the town,
Including the public-houses,
And treated all the cockatoos
And shouted for their spouses.
They danced with all the pretty girls
And held a carnival.
'We don't hurt them who don't hurt us,'
Says Gilbert and Ben Hall.

Australian Homeschooling #563
Successful English 8B

They made a raid on Bathurst,
The pace was getting hot;
But Johnny Vane surrendered
After Micky Burke was shot,
O'Meally at Goimbla did like a hero fall;
'The game is getting lively,'
Says John Gilbert and Ben Hall.

Then Gilbert took a holiday,
Ben Hall got new recruits;
The Old Man and Dunleavy
Shared in the plunder's fruits.
Dunleavy he surrendered
And they jagged the Old Man tall -
So Johnny Gilbert came again
To help his mate Ben Hall.

John Dunn he was a jockey bloke,
A-riding all the winners
Until he joined Hall's gang to rob
The publicans and sinners;
And many a time the Royal Mail
Bailed up at John Dunn's call.
A thousand pounds is on their heads -
Dunn, Gilbert, and Ben Hall.

'Next week we'll visit Goulburn
And clean the banks out there;
So if you see the troopers,
Just tell them to beware;
Some day to Sydney city we mean to pay a call,
And we'll take the whole darn country,'
Says Dunn, Gilbert, and Ben Hall.

A. Answer these questions:

1. Are both poems written as a narrative or as a lyric?

   _____

2. What is the common theme of both poems?

   _____

   _____

3. How is each poem divided up?

   _____

   _____

4. What form of rhyming has been used in "The Wild Colonial Boy"? Has the same type of rhyming been used in "The Ballad of Ben Hall"?

_____

_____

5. Read the chorus again in "The Wild Colonial Boy". What is the line that might sum up the reason that bushrangers may have attained some popularity among the ex-convicts and Irish settlers?

_____

_____

B. Written Expression

Bushrangers were thieves and murderers. While they gained popularity in ballads and poems no-one would really have wanted their coach to be held up by a bushranger. Discuss this statement.

Include:

- the names of the some of the more popular bushrangers
- the reasons they became bushrangers (be realistic)
- whether the bushrangers' actions live up to those outlined in ballads
- were ballads about bushrangers a means of the population expressing "support of the under dog?"
- were ballads in reality popular because they were so easy to sing at a gathering? (Remember there were no radios, televisions, phones or internet.)

Adverbial Clause

Adverbial Clauses are subordinate clauses that do the work of adverbs. They add meaning to verbs, adverbs or adjectives. Like adverbs they tell where, when, how and why. They may also be referred to as clauses of manner, time, place and reason.

For example: Bob walked <u>where the road is cleanest.</u> (where—place)
Mr Smith was sleeping <u>when we arrived.</u> (when—time)
My friend weeded the garden <u>as he was told.</u> (how—manner)
You will find the pattern difficult <u>unless you are an experienced knitter.</u> (why—reason)

Read each sentence. Identify and underline the adverbial clause. Say whether it is a clause of manner, time, place or reason. Be careful you don't miss any.

1. Please visit us whenever you are in Werribee.

          _____

2. "You broke it," Amy said, planting her hands on her hips.

          _____

3. Since I am late for dinner, I will buy a sandwich before I return home.

          _____

4. Olivia can swim better than Joel can.

          _____

5. "This has been an awful day!" said Jill, as the rain poured down her back.

          _____

6. "What a nuisance this rain is," said Mum, as she unpegged her wet washing from the line.

          _____

7. He sowed the carrot seeds where he had prepared the ground.

          _____

8. We sighted Adelaide as we entered St Vincent's Gulf.

          _____

9. Mum ran into the yard when she heard Krystal scream.

          _____

Adverbial Phrase

An adverbial phrase is a group of words that add meaning to the verb. They tell how, when, where or why.

For example: My friend always arrives <u>on time</u>.
The phrase "*on time*" tells when she arrives.

A. Look at each sentence below. Underline the adverbial phrase. On the line provided say whether it tells how, when, where or why. Make sure you don't miss any.

1. Mum will pick us up after school is out. _____

2. He returned to the house for his key. _____

3. The forecast says it will rain all day _____

4. We met Michelle at the shops. _____

5. As we travel John and Michael read their books in the car.

   _____

6. The snake slithered through the grass on his belly.

   _____

7. We raced our bikes down the dirt road. _____

8. We took the country road to avoid the traffic. _____

B. Sometimes it is better to use an adverb instead of a an adverbial phrase. Underline the adverbial phrase. Rewrite the sentence replacing the adverbial phrase with an adverb.

1. The man, without a second's hesitation, raced to the rescue.

   _____

2. Perhaps he will visit me on the day after today.

   _____

3. In the end we will finish laying this path.

   _____

4. My friend arrived at the correct time.

   _____

Rivalry Between France and England in India

In India there was rivalry between the British and French trading stations. There were no colonists. It was a struggle for power to control the Indian rulers after the death of the last great Moghul. Whichever country had the greatest influence over the native rulers would have the greatest commercial advantage.

The British East India Company held trading posts at Bombay, Calcutta, Madras and Surat. The French headquarters were at Pondicherry in the Carnatic, while they had factories at Mahe on the west coast and Chandernagore in Bengal. Both of these companies had come to India originally to trade, but India was in a state of chaos and there was constant rivalry between the various independent states which gave the Europeans an opportunity to interfere.

Francois Dupleix, the French Governor of Pondicherry, began to work to bring the whole of South India under French control. He trained Indian forces and then began intriguing with native princes in order to secure political control over southern India and exclude the British from its trade. In so doing he began an "unofficial war" against Britain that lasted from 1749-54. The English navy under Barnett captured a few French ships. The French Governor besieged Madras in 1746, both by land and sea.

The Treaty of Aix-La-Chapelle in 1748 ended the general war between England and France and, as part of the peace treaty, Madras was restored to the English. The rivalry over possessions in India continued and had to be decided.

Dupleix supported a pro-French candidate as ruler in the Carnatic and also at Hyderabad and he almost succeeded in gaining control of the whole of the Carnatic. The last British stronghold was at Trichinopoly.

At the critical moment when the British seemed likely to be driven out, the position was saved by Robert Clive. Clive gained permission to seize the native capital of Arcot. He captured and held it and by doing so drew off the besiegers from Trichnopoly.

He then defeated the besiegers and slowly overran the whole Carnatic, thus changing the whole situation: for the prestige of the British was restored and the French influence destroyed. Dupleix strove to win back what had been lost, but the French government recalled him in disgrace in 1754 and both Companies agreed to keep the peace.

England won in India for many reasons. The naval superiority of the British allowed the English to move swiftly to and from India. The English Government approved of the policies and programmes of the English Company, whereas the French Government had little interest in Indian affairs.

Britain was in the strongest financial position. This was increased when the English established control over Bengal, one of the richest and most prosperous regions

A. Answer these questions:

1. Why was there a struggle between the British and French in India after the death of the last great Moghul?

_____

_____

2. Other than the death of the Moghul, what was it that gave the French and British the opportunity to interfere in India?

_____

_____

3. Explain how the French went about trying to achieve this control.

_____

_____

4. By 1748 what gains had France made?

_____

5. What changed the situation and gave Britain back a large trading control in India?

_____

_____

_____

_____

6. List the reasons Britain won India.

_____

_____

_____

B. Word Knowledge: choose a word from the text that means the same as each word below.

1. reputation or influence arising from success or achievement

_____

2. the use of underhand scheme to achieve an objective

_____

3. to surround with armed force

_____

C. Find a map of India during this period and locate the areas being discussed.

Word Usage

A. Use a single word instead of the underlined words, rewrite each sentence without changing its meaning.

1. An oil company decided to consult a <u>scientist trained to study the rocks forming the earth's crust.</u>

    _____

2. Leonard da Vinci was noted for his <u>ability to turn readily and successfully from one subject or occupation to another.</u>

    _____

3. He spoke <u>without any variation in the pitch of his voice.</u>

    _____

4. A <u>rule to be followed in future</u> has been established.

    _____

5. Joseph's plans were <u>as hazy as a cloud.</u>

    _____

6. I was commended for my <u>ability to use all available means.</u>

    _____

B. From the clues given find the "disc" word. The first one is completed for you.

1. The disc that housewives like when shopping.   discount

2. The disc that can make a distinction.   _____

3. The disc that allows to be seen or known.   _____

4. The disc that likes clashing sounds or loud noises.   _____

5. The disc that is rude.   _____

6. The disc that appeals to teachers and parents   _____

7. The disc you can throw.   _____

8. The disc that knows the difference between right and wrong.   _____

9. The disc that disturbs   _____

A. Use the suffix –al and –ar to make adjectives from:

1. consul _____   2. element _____

3. title _____   4. universe _____

5. family _____   6. gland _____

7. monument _____   7. office _____

B. Complete the collective nouns.

1. a _____ of islands   2. a _____ of acrobats

3. a _____ of angels   4. a _____ of geese

5. a _____ of directors   6. a _____ of sharks

7. a _____ of dinosaurs   8. a _____ of dolphins

9. a _____ of lions   10. a _____ of bacteria

11. a _____ of stars   12. a _____ of cars

13. a _____ of workmen   14. a _____ of worshippers

C. Write the plural form of the following words:

1. mosquito _____   2. alley _____

3. man-eater _____   4. sister-in-law _____

5. fish _____   6. volcano _____

7. story _____   8. fly _____

9. mercy _____   10. ally _____

11. vertex _____   12. parenthesis _____

13. quiz _____   14. cactus _____

D. Many mistakes come from the similarity in sound or appearance of certain words. Select one of the two words in brackets to fit the definition.

1. to influence   (affect, effect)   _____

2. important   (momentary, momentous)   _____

Australian Poetry Through the Ages: Squatters & Selectors

In Australia, a squatter was a man, either a free settler or ex-convict who occupied a large tract of Crown Land in order to graze livestock. All land was considered Crown Land unless purchased or granted by the Crown. Once a way was found across the Blue Mountains squatters began to spread out with their livestock, often having no legal rights to the land. They gained rights to its usage by being the first Europeans in the area.

From the mid-1820s, however, the occupation of Crown land without legal title became more widespread. As wool began to be exported to England and the colonial population increased, the occupation of pastoral land for raising cattle and sheep progressively became a more lucrative enterprise. The meat market for the population also expanded.

'Squatting' had become so widespread by the mid-1830s that Government policy in the Colony of New South Wales shifted from opposition to the practice to regulation and control. By that stage the term 'squatter' was applied to those who occupied Crown Land under a lease or licence.

Immigration increased during and after the gold rush. The Government started selling small sections of land to those migrants, who were known, as 'selectors,' because they selected their land from a map. This created problems as a squatter might already be using the land and consider it his own.

The following ballads give you a glimpse into this period. Life could be very difficult.

A Squatter's Diary
By Henry E. Butler

Winter's gone, the Spring has come,
Grass is green all over run ;
Autumn lambs are in good nick,
Tiptop market, sell them quick ;
Returns come back, and then I get
Account sales and a good fat cheque.
Go and have a month in town,
Come back, find the run burnt brown,
Ride through run, grass seed here,
Burr in wool, time to shear.
Shearing started yesterday,
Things are now well under way.
Soon machinery all goes wrong,
Another expert sent along.
He gets things right, start again,
Down come twenty points of rain.
Sheep too wet for men to shear,

They must dry for three days clear.
The three days up, sheep brought in,
Shearing starts but stops again ;
Shearers go to boss and say,
Sheep must dry for one more day."
Rouseabouts have four days' spell,
Pay for whole week or there's hell.
Fresh start has been made again,
Wool goes down by every train ;
Six weeks, still more sheep to shear,
One more week then shearers clear;
Rouseabouts tucker, seven weeks' bill,
'Tis indeed a bitter pill.
Settled up with all the men,
Hand quite stiff from using pen ;
Signing cheques is not a joke,
Profits melt at every stroke.
Now the wool has all been sold,
Truly sheep are mints of gold.
Wool all brought a splendid price,
"Topped the market, that was nice.
One can't live in town for ever,
Come back to the never never;"
Tanks and creek are very low,
Must rain soon or stock will go.
No rain yet; call tenders for
Putting down artesian bore.
Bore now down two thousand feet,
Splendid flow, terrific heat.
Paddocks now are eaten bare,
Sheep are dying, here and there ;
Must look after those on hand,
Shift them on to rented land.
Rain at last; the country's saved,
The way to next year's profits paved
Fortune is once more in sight,
Once more prospects looking bright.

Answer the following questions:

1. What is the theme or main idea of the Squatter's Diary?

_____

_____

2. How has the poet used the structure of the lines and the vocabulary to convey the theme and give the impression of time passing?

_____

_____

3. Complete: The poem rhymes in _____.

4. Describe the tone of the poem.

_____

_____

The Free Selector's Daughter

I met her on the Lachlan Side --
A darling girl I thought her,
And ere I left I swore I'd win
The free-selector's daughter.

I milked her father's cows a month,
I brought the wood and water,
I mended all the broken fence,
Before I won the daughter.

I listened to her father's yarns,
I did just what I `oughter',
And what you'll have to do to win
A free-selector's daughter.

I broke my pipe and burnt my twist,
And washed my mouth with water;
I had a shave before I kissed
The free-selector's daughter.

Then, rising in the frosty morn,
I brought the cows for Mary,
And when I'd milked a bucketful
I took it to the dairy.

I poured the milk into the dish
While Mary held the strainer,
I summoned heart to speak my wish,
And, oh! her blush grew plainer.

I told her I must leave the place,
I said that I would miss her;
At first she turned away her face,
And then she let me kiss her.

© Valerie Marett
Coroneos Publications

Australian Homeschooling #563
Successful English 8B

I put the bucket on the ground,
And in my arms I caught her:
I'd give the world to hold again
That free-selector's daughter!

1. What is the theme of the poem?

   _____

   _____

2. Contrast the poem "The Free Selector's Daughter" with "A Squatter's Diary."

   _____

   _____

3. What does the expression "Lachlan Side" refer to?

   _____

   _____

4. Which poem do you prefer? Explain why.

   _____

   _____

   _____

   _____

Research:

Find out more about the Squatters and the Selectors. Include:

- who they were
- why there was constant antagonism between them
- the Government's position
- how the problem was eventually resolved

Give an oral report on what you have discovered.

Sentences

A. Correct the following sentences.

1. It is one of those books that hold your interest throughout.

   _____

2. No-one who has their feet on the ground will ever take themselves too seriously.

   _____

3. To every argument there is at least two sides.

   _____

4. Four weeks' leave have been granted to all workers.

   _____

5. We wasn't surprised at the result, but now he or I are faced with the task of preparing a new plan.

   _____

   _____

6. Each of the men have been told to come prepared for a long journey.

   _____

7. But I am not the person who you are searching for.

   _____

8. It was I whom seen you near the gate in the lane.

   _____

9. A raise in prices and wages usually goes together.

   _____

10. Neither he or I were able to throw any light on the matter.

    _____

11. The committee have reached their decision.

    _____

12. Both of you and me are invited to their party.

    _____

© Valerie Marett
Coroneos Publications

Australian Homeschooling #563
Successful English 8B

Proverbs

Read the proverbs listed in A below. In B you will find a list of proverbs meanings. From list A choose the appropriate proverb and match it with each meaning. Write it in the space provided below each meaning.

A. Proverbs

1. Empty vessels make the most noise.
2. Civility costs nothing.
3. Every cloud has a silver lining.
4. Whilst there's life there's hope.
5. He who pays the piper calls the tune.
6. Nothing ventured, nothing gained.
7. There's many a slip 'twixt the cup and the lip.
8. Jack of all trades, master of none.

B. Meanings

a. There is something good in every unpleasant occurrence.

_____

b. A person who changes his job too often never becomes really expert at anything.

_____

c. So long as one is able to go on trying there is hope of success.

_____

d. You can not be sure that all expectations will be realised.

_____

e. Ignorant people talk more loudly than wise ones.

_____

f. It is no more trouble to be polite than rude.

_____

g. The person who pays the expense of something has the right to decide what is being done.

_____

h. If you don't try, you will never accomplish anything.

_____

Adverbial Clauses and Phrases

An adverbial phrase is a group of words that add meaning to the verb. They tell how, when, where or why.

> For example: My friend always arrives <u>on time</u>.
> The phrase "*on time*" tells when she arrives.

Adverbial clauses are subordinate clauses that do the work of adverbs. They add meaning to verbs, adverbs or adjectives. Like adverbs they tell where, when, how and why. They may also be referred to as clauses of manner, time, place and reason.

> For example: Bob walked <u>where the road is cleanest.</u> (where—place)

A. **Underline the adverbial clause and say whether it is a clause of manner, time, place or reason.**

1. They walked next to the stream that bubbled over stones. _____

2. He won the race because he trained so hard. _____

3. When we reached the spring we drank thirstily. _____

4. Keep your shoulders back and down as the trainer always tells you. _____

5. "We are lost," groaned John, as he peered at the map. _____

B. Underline the adverbial phrase and say whether it is a phrase of manner, time, place or reason.

1. He tipped the sand in the middle of the path. _____

2. We refused the invitation for medical reasons. _____

3. Early in the morning the air is cold and fresh. _____

4. Our grandparents will arrive in about half an hour in a taxi. _____

5. Sandra and Peter must walk home on the path. _____

C. Each sentence contains either an adverbial phrase or an adverbial clause. Identify it. Write it on the line provided and say if it is a phrase or a clause.

1. I went to bed very early because I was very tired.

   _____

2. We shall be late for the concert if we do not hurry.

   _____

3. Unfortunately the ball was kicked over the line.

   _____

4. After I've eaten I will give my room a good clean.

   _____

5. The great shark swam silently below the sea.

   _____

6. We shall be late for the concert if you do not hurry.

   _____

D. Each sentence below contains either an adverbial clause or an adjectival clause. Write the clause on the line provided and say if it is an adjectival or adverbial clause.

1. The thieves robbed the home while the family were on holiday.

   _____

2. Tell me about the place which you are visiting.

   _____

3. Please arrange the books so I can still see you.

   _____

4. How is your friend for whom you baked a cake?

   _____

5. We played on the beach until the sun set.

   _____

6. My house is not as large as Peter's is.

   _____

Changes in Europe: The French Revolution Begins

The ideas from the French Revolution had, in one form or another, passed through most European political systems. The Revolution challenged the old order of things in France. Before the Revolution the monarchy was absolute. During the Revolution Louis XVI was reduced to a constitutional monarch and finally, on January 21st, 1793 he was beheaded.

Up until this time France had three distinct classes within society. The King was an absolute monarch and was believed to have been given the right by God to rule absolutely and should be obeyed. The "First Estate" was made up of the clergy who ran the church and some aspects of the country and had power to levy a 10% tax. The nobility made up the "Second Estate," and included all members of the royal family except the King. The nobility and clergy were not required to pay taxes. The "Third Estate" included the remaining members of society who paid most of the tax. This was in addition to the tax to the clergy.

Various groups appeared at this time. One of these, the Montagnards, a Jacobin group who wanted to gain control of the masses, was prepared to pursue a loose welfare-state policy favouring the "have nots" against the "haves"— the masses against the aristocracy. They attacked the old feudal system and the idea of the Divine Right of Kings. The United States was later set up under these ideas.

There were so many grievances and so many different political ideas that the Royal Court treated the matter lightly. The monarchy, clergy and nobility did not want to grant those below them any equality or tax relief and, since the "Third Estate" was so disunited, underestimated its power.

A National Assembly was formed on June 17th, 1789, but not approved by Louis XVI. It was to remain in power until a new constitution could be written and passed. One of the results of the King ignoring the situation was the storming of the Bastille on July 14th, 1789 by a group of tradesmen and salesmen who managed to steal weapons. This soon turned into a mob and included soldiers who had deserted. The Bastille, a prison in Paris, represented the monarchy to the people. The Marquis de Launay, who was in charge of the prison, attempted to negotiate, expecting the King to send reinforcements. However these negotiations ended when more of the revolutionaries entered the Bastille. The soldiers fired and two hundred people were killed. The rest of the mob stormed the Bastille, overrunning and killing the soldiers and beheading the Marquis de Launay. This was the beginning of the ruling by the mob in Paris and the end of the nobility as rulers.

The Army could not control the situation so a National Guard was set up on 15th July, 1789. It was led by La Fayette, a wealthy member of society and a hero of the American War of Independence. On July 11, 1789 La Fayette proposed a declaration of rights to the French National Assembly that he had modelled on the American Declaration of Independence. He later refused to support the escalation of violence, known as the Reign of Terror, that followed the French royal family's attempt to flee the country in 1791. This resulted in his imprisonment as a traitor from 1792 to 1797.

A. Answer these questions:

1. Briefly outline the three distinct classes or Estates in France during this period.

   _____

   _____

   _____

2. What is meant by the Divine Right of Kings? (Do some research to make sure you understand this concept.)

   _____

   _____

3. Having read the text what do you imagine was the biggest complaint of the Third Estate?

   _____

   _____

4. How did this discontent first show itself? (Be careful you answer fully.)

   _____

   _____

5. Did the mob rule stop after the storming of the Bastille? If not what measures were undertaken to bring stability to the situation?

   _____

   _____

   _____

6. From your reading of the text, why do you think La Fayette was only imprisoned and not guillotined when he fell out of popularity?

   _____

   _____

B. Word Knowledge: choose a word from the text that means the same as each definition below.

1. a class or body regarded as forming one of the social structures of a country   _____

2. a large crowd of people, especially one that is intent on causing trouble or violence   _____

Australian Poetry Through the Ages: Stockmen

A **stockman** was a person who looked after the livestock on a large property known as a station. These were owned by squatters or graziers. Stockmen who worked with cattle in the Top End were known as **ringers** and were often only employed for the dry season which lasted from April to October. A **station hand** was an employee, who was involved in routine duties on a station and, at times, this involved caring for livestock.

Stockmen and drovers, known as **overlanders**, developed pride in the skills which required them to drive sheep and cattle over long distances. This is reflected in the ballads about them.

Most Australian bushmen had a dry sense of humour. They were aware of the dangers in the land around them and the changes in seasons. This was also reflected in the ballads about them.

Andy's Gone with Cattle

by Henry Lawson

Our Andy's gone to battle now
'Gainst Drought, the red marauder;
Our Andy's gone with cattle now
Across the Queensland border.

He's left us in dejection now,
Our thoughts with him are roving;
It's dull on this selection now,
Since Andy went a-droving.

Who now shall wear the cheerful face
In times when things are slackest?
And who shall whistle round the place
When Fortune frowns her blackest?

Oh, who shall cheek the squatter now
When he comes round us snarling?
His tongue is growing hotter now
Since Andy crossed the Darling.

The gates are out of order now,
In storms the 'riders' rattle;
For far across the border now
Our Andy's gone with cattle.

Poor Aunty's looking thin and white;
And Uncle's cross with worry;
And poor old Blucher howls all night
Since Andy left Macquarie.

Oh, may the showers in torrents fall,
And all the tanks run over;
And may the grass grow green and tall
In pathways of the drover;

And may good angels send the rain
On desert stretches sandy;
And when the summer comes again
God grant 'twill bring us Andy.

Read the poem carefully then answer the questions below. Answer in sentences.

1. What caused Andy to leave?

   _____

   _____

2. Where did Andy live? How do we know this?

   _____

   _____

3. Why does Lawson wish that '*the showers in torrents fall, and all the tanks run over*'?

   _____

4. What are the results of Andy leaving as described in the poem?

   _____

   _____

   _____

   _____

5. What structural features are used, e.g., rhyming patterns, number of lines?

   _____

   _____

6. Read the poem again carefully. Who is the person speaking through the poem? Why do you think so?

   _____

   _____

The poem on the next page reflects the awareness of people at this time of the ever present dangers of the bush and droving. The author is unknown.

© Valerie Marett
Coroneos Publications

Australian Homeschooling #563
Successful English 8B

The Dying Stockman

A strapping young stockman lay dying,
His saddle supporting his head;
His two mates around him were crying,
As he rose on his elbow and said:

Chorus: 'Wrap me up with my stockwhip and blanket,
And bury me deep down below,
Where the dingoes and crows can't molest me,
In the shade where the coolibahs grow.

'Oh! had I the flight of the bronzewing,
Far o'er the plains would I fly,
Straight to the land of my childhood,
And there I would lay down and die.

Chorus:

'Then cut down a couple of saplings,
Place one at my head and my toe,
Carve on them cross, stockwhip, and saddle,
To show there's a stockman below.

Chorus:

'Hark! there's the wail of a dingo,
Watchful and weird - I must go,
For it tolls the death-knell of the stockman
From the gloom of the scrub down below.

Chorus:

'There's tea in the battered old billy;
Place the pannikins out in a row,
And we'll drink to the next merry meeting,
In the place where all good fellows go.

Chorus:

'And oft in the shades of the twilight,
When the soft winds are whispering low,
And the darkening shadows are falling,
Sometimes think of the stockman below.'

Read the poem carefully then answer the questions below. Notice that death is accepted as a normal, if unfortunate, occurrence. Answer in sentences.

1. Write the meaning of the following words:

   a. coolibah:_____

b. bronzewing: _____

c. saplings: _____

d. pannikins: _____

2. While the ballad does not speak specifically of the landscape around the dying stockman we can still draw our own conclusions. What do you think the landscape was like? Explain why you think this.

_____

_____

_____

3. What is the format of the poem?

_____

_____

4. Most ballads had catchy tunes. "The Dying Stockman" was often sung to the tune of "Botany Bay." Why do you think the tunes were usually catchy? What have been the advantages of a catchy tune with a ballad like "The Dying Stockman?"

_____

_____

_____

This last ballad is totally different. It contains more imagery. Read it and think about it before answering the questions.

The Stockman
By David Campbell

The sun was in the summer grass
The coolibahs were twisted steel:
The stockman paused beneath its shade
And sat upon his heel,
And with the rein looped through his arm
He rolled tobacco in his palm.

His horse stood still. His cattle dog
Tongued in the shadow of the tree,
And for a moment on the plain
Time waited for the three.
And then the stockman licked his fag
And Time took up his solar swag.

I saw the stockman mount and ride
Across the mirage on the plain;

And still the timeless moment brought
Fresh ripples to my brain:
It seemed in that distorting air
I saw his grandson sitting there.

Answer these questions:

1. Explain the following metaphors:

   a. The sun was in the summer grass.

   _____

   b. The coolabahs were twisted steel

   _____

2. What has been personified in this poem? Explain how this has been done.

   _____

   _____

3. Explain "his cattle dog tongued."

   _____

   _____

4. What is a mirage?

   _____

5. How did the mirage change the view? How does this fit into the context of the poem?

   _____

   _____

6. Explain the rhyming of the poem.

   _____

   _____

7. The poem gives us an impression of the day being hot. Do you agree? Explain why or why not.

   _____

   _____

   _____

Malapropisms

A malapropism is a ludicrous misuse of a word. Replace the malapropism in italics with the correct word from the box. Learn any words you do not know.

> monogamy, prodigy, credible, optimistic, emphatic, masticate, invention, amphibious, debut, equivocal, insecticide, sonatas

1. Beethoven was an infant *progeny*; he composed three *tomatoes* before he was four years old.

   _____

   _____

2. His denial of the charges was so *erratic* that everybody believed him.

   _____

3. Since a frog lives on both land and water he is classified as *ambiguous.*

   _____

4. Some of the adventures he claimed to have were hardly *creditable.*

   _____

5. In this country a man can have only one wife. This is called *monotony.*

   _____

6. The man's *equivalent* replies aroused police suspicion.

   _____

7. Necessity is the mother of *intervention.*

   _____

8. *Infanticide* is an excellent way of getting rid of household pests.

   _____

9. John was *octopus*, always expecting something good to turn up.

   _____

10. You will have indigestion if you do not *emasculate* your food properly.

    _____

11. The actors *debacle* was made at fifteen.

    _____

Clauses and Phrase

A. Each sentence below contains an underlined portion. Say whether the underlined portion is a clause or phrase.

1. <u>After listening to the examiner's instructions</u>, the class began the test.

   _____

2. <u>If you have solved the problem</u>, here's a harder one.

   _____

3. <u>I was grounded for two weeks</u> because of the broken window.

   _____

4. <u>Opening the mail,</u> Mrs Jones found an invitation to a party.

   _____

5. After he had finished his dinner <u>Johnathon climbed the stairs to bed.</u>

   _____

6. Watermelon, a refreshing fruit, is nice to eat <u>on a hot day</u>.

   _____

B. Read each sentence below. Identify the subordinate clause.

1. Since we expected crowds, we planned to arrive early at the show.

   _____

2. You will like Phillip Island penguin parade if you like penguins.

   _____

3. The ambulance, that carried the sick man, raced to the hospital.

   _____

4. Since she has seen the movie twice, Olivia was a fan of dinosaurs.

   _____

5. Jason got drenched as he waited in the rain at the bus stop.

   _____

6. If you come to my house I will help you with your homework.

   _____

Sentences

A. Rewrite the sentences adding the correct punctuation.

1. My icecream which is chocolate flavoured is melting fast

_____

2. Although I don't want to get sunburnt I like laying outside on the grass

_____

3. I would like to invite you to my party my friend Veronica said

_____

4. I bought new shorts sunglasses a swimsuit and tank tops for a holiday at the beach.

_____

_____

B. Combine the two sentences in every question below to make a complex sentence. Make each sentence as concise as possible.

1. The highschool band gave a concert. It lasted for an hour.

_____

2. We waited for Frank. We waited for David. We waited for Peter.

_____

3. When you draw a clown, be sure to give it a funny nose. Also give it huge eyes. Then give it a big mouth.

_____

4. Mum went to speak to our neighbour. Our neighbour lives across the street.

_____

5. We reached the spring. We drank thirstily.

_____

6. Mr Dexter is my piano teacher. He has been teaching me for three years.

_____

Changes in Europe: Declaration of the Rights of Man

After the storming of the Bastille, turmoil continued in Paris. Amidst occasional rioting over food shortages, a hundred and eighty members, nominated by the city districts, constituted themselves as legislators and representatives of the city, but had no clear structure. The committees, the mayor, the assembly of representatives, and the individual districts each claimed authority independent of the others. The increasingly middle-class National Guard under Lafayette also slowly emerged as a power in its own right. Other self-generated assemblies arose which felt free to debate the same issues as the National Assembly, to take positions more radically revolutionary than that Assembly, and to try to influence its decisions.

Using the United States Declaration of Independence as a model, on August 26, 1789 the Assembly published the **Declaration of the Rights of Man**. Like the U.S. Declaration, it comprised a statement of principles rather than a constitution with legal effect.

Where the U.S. Declaration had singled out "life, liberty, and the pursuit of happiness" as inalienable rights, the French document opted for "liberty, property, safety, and resistance against oppression." The declaration saw law as an "expression of the general will", intended to promote this equality of rights and to forbid "only actions harmful to the society." It included the need to provide for defence and stated some broad principles about taxation. It also specified a public right to an accounting from public agents.

It did nothing to establish a form of government. For the time, the National Constituent Assembly, its membership drawn from the States General, functioned as a legislature. The Assembly sat continuously, so as not to give the king the time to organise against them. France was to have a single, unicameral Assembly.

While the Assembly moved in the direction of a constitution, the King continued to attempt to resist the Declaration. On the pretext of protecting itself against the Parisian mob, the Court summoned troops to Versailles, doubled the household guards, and sent for the dragoons and the Flanders regiment.

The Assembly divided France into eighty-three départements, uniformly administered and nearly equal to one another in extent and population, replacing the historic provinces. Multi-round elections providing a broad electoral franchise in the first round, but in a subsequent round franchise was limited by property requirements. This effectively abolished the local parliaments, and angered many of the nobility and the bishops.

On August 11, 1789 the tithes were declared suppressed and no equivalent was provided and in December 2, 1789 the enormous land holdings of the Roman Catholic Church were confiscated. The state said it would now provide for the expenses of the Church, including hospitals. A new paper currency was introduced to use the money from the Churches. The Pope never accepted the new arrangement, and it led to a schism in the Church, between those clergy who swore the required oath and those who did not.

A. **Word Knowledge: choose a word from the text that means the same as each definition below.**

1. having a single legislative chamber _____

2. rights that are not able to be taken or given away _____

3. a split or division between strongly opposed sections or parties, caused by differences in opinion or belief _____

4. one tenth of annual earnings taken for support of the Church or clergy _____

5. the right to vote in public elections _____

B. **Answer these questions:**

1. What important document was signed in France during this period? When was it published?

_____

_____

2. Think. What was happening in Australia during this period?

_____

_____

3. What was the document modelled on?

_____

_____

4. Think hard. In your own words summarise how the documents in the U.S.A. and France differed.

_____

_____

5. How was the Catholic Church affected by developments at this time?

_____

_____

Research: Do some research on how, in reality the acts against the Church have affected society in general. Write at least a half page answer.

Australian Poetry Through the Ages: Sheep

For much of its history Australia depended on wool as its main export, and so the notion arose that Australia was 'riding on the sheep's back'. Although wool is now less important as an export, the phrase still evokes a sense of the importance of the agricultural industry to the country's wealth.

In view of this it is not surprising that there were many ballads that mention sheep. The most popular of these "Waltzing Matilda," was for many years played at International Events as an Australian anthem. Another popular one is "Click Go the Shears" which is written below.

Click Go The Shears

Out on the board the old shearer stands,
Grasping his shears in his thin bony hands;
Fixed is his eye on a bare-bellied yoe
Glory if he gets her, won't he make the ringer go.

Chorus:
Click go the shears boys, click, click, click,
Wide is his blow and his hands move quick,
The ringer looks around and is beaten by a blow,
And curses the old snagger with the bare-bellied yoe.

In the middle of the floor in his cane-bottomed chair
Sits the boss of the board with his eyes everywhere,
Notes well each fleece as it comes to the screen,
Paying strict attention that it's taken off clean.

Chorus:

The tar-boy is there waiting in demand
With his blackened tar-pot, in his tarry hand,
Spies one old sheep with a cut upon its back,
Hears what he's waiting for it's "Tar here, Jack!"

Chorus:

Shearing is all over and we've all got our cheques,
Roll up your swags for we're off on the tracks;
The first pub we come to, it's there we'll have a spree,
And everyone that comes along it's, '"come and drink with me!'

Chorus:

Answer these questions:

1. What is the format of the poem?

_____

_____

2. Find words in the poem that fit the following definitions:

   a. person who is the fastest shearer in the shed _____

   b. sheep with little or no wool on its belly _____

   c. young boy who has a bucket of melted tar
      to brush an accidental cut to the sheep
      to stop the sheep bleeding badly _____

   d. rolled up bedding containing all of the
      shearer's possessions _____

   e. person in overall charge _____

   f. old shearer _____

3. What is the tone of this poem?

   _____

   _____

There are many versions of "Waltzing Matilda" ballad. The most popular version was written by Banjo Patterson in 1895. You will find it below.

Waltzing Matilda
By Banjo Patterson

Oh there once was a swagman camped by the billabongs,
Under the shade of a Coolibah tree;
And he sang as he looked at the old billy boiling
"Who'll come a-waltzing Matilda with me."

Chorus:

Who'll come a-waltzing Matilda, my darling.
Who'll come a-waltzing Matilda with me.
Waltzing Matilda and leading a water-bag.
Who'll come a-waltzing Matilda with me.

Up came the jumbuck to drink at the waterhole,
Up jumped the swagman and grabbed him with glee;
And he sang as he put him away in his tucker-bag,
"Who'll come a-waltzing Matilda with me."

Chorus:

Up came the squatter a-riding his thoroughbred;
Up came the policeman - one, two, and three.
Whose is the jumbuck you've got in the tucker-bag?
"You'll come a-waltzing Matilda with we."

Chorus:

Up sprang the swagman and jumped into the waterhole,
Drowning himself by the Coolibah tree;
And his voice can be heard as it sings in the billabongs,
Who'll come a-waltzing Matilda with me."

Chorus:

Answer these questions:

1. What was "Matilda?"

   _____

   _____

2. How has "Matilda" been personified? What is the poet describing when he does this?

   _____

   _____

3. Fill in the gaps:

   a. a jumbuck is a another way of describing a _____.

   b. a billabong is _____

   c. a tucker-bag was a _____.

4. Think! Why do you think the swagman drowned himself?

   _____

   _____

5. What do most ballads rhythm have in common?

   _____

6. On reading the poem our sympathy is with the swagman. This sympathy can be found In many ballads. Why do you think this is?

   _____

   _____

   _____

Find other poems about sheep and read them.

Examples: The Sheep Washer's Lament
           The Shepherd

© Valerie Marett
Coroneos Publications

Australian Homeschooling #563
Successful English 8B

More Malapropisms

A malapropism is the misuse of a word in mistake for one resembling it. The underlined word in each sentence below is a malapropisms. Rewrite the sentence using the correct word.

1. The kennel owner was highly **diluted** when his dog won first prize.

   _____

2. Since time **immaterial** men have striven to better their situation.

   _____

3. A lot of people were **gelatined** during the French Revolution.

   _____

4. Keep the rope **taught** or the tent will fall.

   _____

5. He lost marks because most of his material in his essay was **irreverent.**

   _____

6. He was a **border** at school, for five years.

   _____

7. The speaker told the students he could not too strongly **extort** them to deal with others in a **sportive** manner.

   _____

   _____

8. The coach said he was **adverse** to making any changes in the team.

   _____

9. It is beyond my **apprehension** how you can believe that.

   _____

10. I **resemble** that remark. It is just not true!

    _____

11. I am **injured** to my husband's jokes.

    _____

12. He **extorted** the boy to do his best.

    _____

Noun Clauses

A noun clause, which does the work of a noun:

1.   **may be**

   a.   **the subject of a verb**
   e.g., _Whatever our captain says_ receives instant obedience.

   b.   **the object of a verb or a preposition**
   e.g., The captain decides _who will open the innings._

   c.   **in apposition with a noun or a pronoun in either the nominative or the objective case**
   e.g., The news _that the island had surrendered_ was followed by an announcement _that the victorious troops would receive three weeks leave._

N.B. Apposition is a grammatical construction in which two elements, normally noun phrases, are placed side by side, with one element serving to identify the other in a different way. The two elements are said to be **in apposition**.

2.   **may be**

   a.   **a subordinate conjunction** (that or whether)

   b.   **an interrogative pronoun or adjective** (as, who, whoever, whom, whose, which, what, whatever)

   c.   **an adverbial conjunction** (such as how, when, where or why)

Write the noun clause under each sentence.

1.   What my brother enjoys most is playing football.

   _____

2.   She explained why she couldn't come to the party.

   _____

3.   Mr Scott assigned whoever was late extra homework.

   _____

4.   The club will give whoever wins the race a gold cup.

   _____

5.   What I wonder is why he did it.

   _____

A. Find the noun clauses. Write them in the space provided. State what purpose they serve.

1. He said that he would not go.

   _____

2. I can not rely on what he says.

   _____

3. It is certain that we will have to admit defeat.

   _____

4. That he is not interested in the offer is known to us.

   _____

5. He said that he was not feeling well.

   _____

6. The news that he is alive has been confirmed.

   _____

7. I don't know where he has gone.

   _____

8. It was fortunate that he was present.

   _____

B. Change the questions to a noun clause. The first one is completed for you.

1. What time is it?
   I would like to know _what time it is._

2. When is Mother's Day?

   _____

3. Whose car is this?

   _____

4. What time did the flight arrive?

   _____

5. Why couldn't she catch the bus on time?

   _____

Further Changes in France

By 1792 a Legislative Assembly had been formed. This still only represented ten percent of the population. The peasants did not feel the revolution had gone far enough and frequently caused problems.

The New Assembly had 745 members, a little over half of which were royalist in outlook. About 100 were independents, who held the balance of power and the rest were radicals. In theory France was still a constitutional monarchy.

Europe was afraid that war was coming. Emigres' who had moved to Austria were agitating for it. The New Assembly tried to whip up national feeling by ordering these emigres' be returned to France. In return Leopold II, Emperor of Austria responded with the Declaration of Pillnitz promising to restore Louis XVI to the throne if all the other nations would support him.

Brissot declared in the National Assembly that France could not tolerate Leopold's Declaration and in April 1792 war was declared. France now faced not just one country but also Prussia and its allies who had united with Austria in expectation of war. The French Army was hopelessly disunited and fled from the first encounter and the European army expected a swift victory.

In August 1792 the European Army began an advance, taking towns on the way to Paris. On reaching the outskirts of Paris, as the battle seemed won, the French artillery, which had the reputation as the best in Europe, fired and with the aid of an infantry attack, forced the approaching army to retreat. Ten days later, without firing another shot, the invading army withdrew and with the general advance of the French troops, drove them out of France.

There was trouble in Paris as a result of the war, which the Assembly tried to repress. For a while the Assembly was almost back to the ideas of the Declaration of the Rights of Man. In theory the Assembly was democratic, but in practice they were afraid of the workers and peasants.

Groups developed within the Assembly, none of which made any attempt to compromise. Each side accused the other of treachery, weakness and compromise.

Louis XVI became the political pawn in a struggle between the two strongest factions. Food was in short supply and the Jacobins wanted him brought to trial, alleging the king received better conditions than the people of Paris. The king was tried, found guilty, sentenced to death and executed in January 1793. His wife, Marie Antoinette, was executed not long after. All of their children except one, a girl, died in prison.

A reign of terror took place between 1793 and 1794 and was directed by the Committee of Public Safety, which was instituted to rule in a time of national emergency. They had absolute power and many people were executed during this time.

A. Answer these questions:

1. Why do you think this period in history is often described as "the Reign of Terror? List your reasons.

   _____

   _____

2. Describe what happened when France demanded the emigres', who had fled to Austria, be returned. (Don't miss anything.)

   _____

   _____

   _____

   _____

3. Did the National Assembly, which had effectively replaced the monarchy, work well? Explain your answer.

   _____

   _____

4. Explain what "Louis was a political pawn" means.

   _____

   _____

B. Word Knowledge: choose a word or words from the text that means the same as each definition below.

1. favouring extreme social or political reforms   _____

2. the settlement of a difference by giving way on both sides   _____

3. distribution of power within a government; group holding majority of power   _____

4. form of Government in which a king or queen acts as head of state   _____

5. trying to get public support for something   _____

C. Grammar: identify the subject and predicate in the following sentence.

By 1792 a Legislative Assembly had been formed.

_____

Australian Poetry Through the Ages: Gold

Gold was discovered very early after settlement but it was felt it best to supress the find to prevent convicts revolting. The real gold rushes in Australia began in 1851.

With the gold rush came gold fever. Almost every young man, and some older ones, dropped everything and went looking for a fortune. Squatters lost most of their shepherds, fencers left the big properties, and few shearers were left to do the work. The stories spread that gold was there just lying in the river and creek beds. People from all over the world made for Australia. Crews of ships deserted and ships were left rotting in harbours.

Initially the gold was alluvial and many found gold, but most spent it as fast as they found it. The real winners were the carters who brought the food to the gold-fields, the shopkeepers and the hotel owners, who had a thriving trade. By the end of the gold strikes most people who had come from overseas were forced to stay and find work, not having the money to go home. This boost in immigration helped Australia immensely.

The poems that appear over the next few pages were both written by Henry Lawson. Henry Lawson, who lived from 17 June 1867 – 2 September 1922, was an Australian writer and poet. Along with his contemporary Banjo Paterson, Lawson is among the best-known Australian poets and fiction writers of the colonial period and is often called Australia's "greatest short story writer".

Read the following poem. It is quite long but worth studying in its entirety. The roaring days is another name for the goldrushes.

The Roaring Days

*The night too quickly passes
And we are growing old,
So let us fill our glasses
And toast the Days of Gold;
When finds of wondrous treasure
Set all the South ablaze,
And you and I were faithful mates
All through the roaring days!*

*Then stately ships came sailing
From every harbour's mouth,
And sought the land of promise
That beaconed in the South;
Then southward streamed their streamers
And swelled their canvas full
To speed the wildest dreamers
E'er borne in vessel's hull.*

Their shining Eldorado,
Beneath the southern skies,
Was day and night for ever
Before their eager eyes.
The brooding bush, awakened,
Was stirred in wild unrest,
And all the year a human stream
Went pouring to the West.

The rough bush roads re-echoed
The bar-room's noisy din,
When troops of stalwart horsemen
Dismounted at the inn.
And oft the hearty greetings
And hearty clasp of hands
Would tell of sudden meetings
Of friends from other lands.

And when the cheery camp-fire
Explored the bush with gleams,
The camping-grounds were crowded
With caravans of teams;
Then home the jests were driven,
And good old songs were sung,
And choruses were given
The strength of heart and lung.

Oft when the camps were dreaming,
And fires began to pale,
Through rugged ranges gleaming
Would come the Royal Mail.
Behind six foaming horses,
And lit by flashing lamps,
Old Cobb and Co., in royal state,
Went dashing past the camps.

Oh, who would paint a goldfield,
And paint the picture right,
As old Adventure saw it
In early morning's light?
The yellow mounds of mullock
With spots of red and white,
The scattered quartz that glistened
Like diamonds in light;

The azure line of ridges,
The bush of darkest green,
The little homes of calico
That dotted all the scene.
The flat straw hats with ribands
That old engravings show -
The dress that still reminds us
Of sailors, long ago.

Australian Homeschooling #563
Successful English 8B

I hear the fall of timber
From distant flats and fells,
The pealing of the anvils
As clear as little bells,
The rattle of the cradle,
The clack of windlass-boles,
The flutter of the crimson flags
Above the golden holes.
Ah, then their hearts were bolder,

And if Dame Fortune frowned
Our swags we'd lightly shoulder
And tramp to other ground.
Oh, they were lion-hearted
Who gave our country birth!
Stout sons, of stoutest fathers born,
From all the lands on earth!

Those golden days are vanished,
And altered is the scene;
The diggings are deserted,
The camping-grounds are green;
The flaunting flag of progress
Is in the West unfurled,
The mighty bush with iron rails
Is tethered to the world.

Answer these questions:

1. Who or what is Eldorado? What image does this conjure up in your mind?

   _____

   _____

   _____

2. What words has Lawson used to describe the number of people heading for the goldfields? What images does this suggest to you?

   _____

   _____

3. Explain the following:

   a. Royal Mail: _____

   _____

   b. Cobb and Co.:_____

   _____

4. Henry Lawson has used personification twice in this poem. Explain where he has used it and why? Has it added to the poem? Explain your answer.

_____

_____

_____

5. Henry Lawson has given us some vivid pictures of the scenery and the people. Give 3 examples from different verses.

_____

_____

6. Henry Lawson has used adjectives, adverbs and phrases freely to enhance the general picture he is painting of the goldfields. Give examples and explain how you feel these have contributed to the poem.

_____

_____

_____

_____

7. Explain the lines, "*The mighty bush with iron rails, Is tethered to the world.*"

_____

_____

Further Work:

Prepare a report on life on the goldfields. Do the majority of your research in a library and not on the internet.

Include:

- living conditions

- type of food available

- trades that supported the goldfields

- presence, or not, of women and children

- accommodation

- nationalities present

Noun Phrase

A Noun Phrase is a word or group of words containing a noun and functioning in a sentence as subject, object, or prepositional object.

For example: I like **singing** <u>in the bath.</u>
<u>Our</u> **friend** has bought a house next door.

A. Identify the noun phrase in each sentence. Write it in the space provided.

1. Has anyone seen the back door key?

   _____

2. She is my favourite sports teacher.

   _____

3. I picked the dark horse to win the race.

   _____

4. I hope to be there in time.

   _____

5. The jury believed the man guilty.

   _____

6. The children were surprised by the summer rain.

   _____

7. We were excited about the sports carnival.

   _____

8. I don't have a bank account.

   _____

B. State if the underlined words are a noun phrase or a noun clause.

1. I heard <u>that he had succeeded</u>.   _____

2. Nobody knows <u>why he failed.</u>   _____

3. <u>His arrival</u> was totally unexpected.   _____

4. I know <u>that he is trustworthy.</u>   _____

5. He confessed <u>his guilt.</u>   _____

Choosing Better Words

One word in each sentence is underlined. Below each sentence four words are given. Select the better word and rewrite the sentence.

1. Our building was in urgent need of <u>renewal.</u>
    a. accessories   b. extra space   c. improvement   d. renovation

    _____

2. Our team fought <u>unyieldingly</u> for victory.
    a. unselfishly   b. tenaciously   c. unwillingly   d. bravely

    _____

3. Only the most <u>disbelieving</u> people were unconvinced.
    a. hygienic   b. sarcastic   c. sceptical   d. regal

    _____

4. My mother gave me only a <u>passing</u> glance as I entered the room.
    a. interested   b. cursory   c. impatient   d. condescending

    _____

5. Your history essay contains too much <u>non-essential</u> material.
    a. useful   b. prejudiced   c. incriminating   d. extraneous

    _____

6. <u>Provisional</u> arrangements had been made for the Scout camp.
    a. tentative   b. later   c. early   suitable

    _____

7. A giggle arose which the teacher <u>stilled</u> with a glance.
    a. acknowledged   b. evaluated   c. quelled   d. over-looked

    _____

8. The debater's <u>misleading</u> arguments did not deceive the adjudicator.
    a. logical   b. extensive   c. sincere   d. fallacious

9. On account of his position in the community his story was given wide <u>belief.</u>
    a. acclaim   b. credence   c. publicity   d. attention

    _____

10. Honesty was one of our Prime Minister's most <u>prominent</u> traits.
    a. most admirable   b. basic   c. salient   d. inherent

    _____

The Terror 1793-4

In July 1793 the Revolution was struggling. The British Navy hovered outside French ports waiting to connect with the enemy force advancing on France. Within France the revolutionary groups were disunited. The ordinary peasants and trades people in Paris, known as the sans-culottes, were prone to riot over food shortages.

The Committee of Public Safety were the ones who marshalled the nation's forces to meet the many crises. Marat was dead, but people were still following his idea that only the extreme use of the guillotine against traitors, suspects and counter-revolutionaries would solve the nation's problems.

On September 4th 1793 a demonstration for more wages and bread was quickly turned into a call for "terror". This was continued on 5th when the sans-culottes marched to speak to the Committee. Chaumette, backed by thousands of sans-culottes, declared that the Committee should tackle the shortages by a strict implementation of the laws. The Committee agreed and, in addition, voted to finally organise the revolutionary armies to march against the hoarders and unpatriotic members of the countryside.

In addition Danton, another leading figure, argued that arms production should be increased until every patriot had a musket, and that the Revolutionary Tribunal should be divided so as to make it work faster. The sans-culottes had once again forced their wishes through; terror was now in force.

Over the following weeks radical action was taken. On September 17th a Law of Suspects was introduced allowing for the arrest of anyone whose conduct suggested they were supporters of tyranny or federalism, a law which could be easily twisted to affect just about everyone in the nation. A maximum price was set for a wide range of food and goods. The Revolutionary Armies was formed and sent out to search for traitors and crush revolt.

Some good laws were passed during this period. The Bocquier Law of December 19th, 1793 provided a system of compulsory and free state education for all children aged 6 – 13 years old, albeit with a curriculum stressing patriotism. Homeless children became a state responsibility, and people born out of wedlock were given full inheritance rights. A universal system of metric weights and measurements was introduced on August 1st, 1793, while an attempt to end poverty was made by using property owned by suspects to aid the poor.

Around half a million people were imprisoned across France, and approximately 10,000 were in prison without trial. However, this early phase of the terror was not aimed at nobles. Most executions occurred in Federalist areas after the army had regained control and some loyal areas escaped largely unscathed.

Deputies on mission began attacking the symbols of Catholicism: smashing images, vandalising buildings and burning vestments. A revolutionary calendar was introduced with twelve, thirty day months, with three ten day weeks, starting on September 22nd, 1792. This continued the dechristianisation.

A. Answer these questions:

1. Think! State in your own words why, by July 1793, the Revolution was struggling.

   _____

   _____

   _____

2. Who was the real ruling party at this time?

   _____

3. Who were the sans-culottes? Why did they have so much influence?

   _____

   _____

4. What were the most positive results from the demands made by the sans-culottes on the Committee on 4th September, 1793?

   _____

   _____

   _____

5. Briefly explain what was contained in Bocquier's Law.

   _____

   _____

   _____

6. The Catholic Church as a whole in France was very rich and supported the invasion by the European nations. What steps were made against the Church during this period?

   _____

   _____

B. Word Knowledge: choose a word or words from the text that means the same as each definition below.

1. even though   _____

2. A system of government where power is divided between a central authority and states or boroughs.   _____

3. oppressive power   _____

Australian Poetry Through the Ages: Gold 2

Henry Lawson's poems often speak of the harsh realities experienced by poor country folk. "*Eureka*" and "*The Fight at Eureka Stockade*", both by Henry Lawson, reveal the event that changed Australian history.

When gold fever hit Australia almost every young man, and some older ones, dropped everything and went looking for a fortune. People from all over the world headed to Australia. The Government required the miners to have a licence to mine. The Government raised the price of a Miner's Right to about £1 a week. Many miners could not afford this.

The Victorian Governor had lost most of his Police force to the diggings. The towns sprung up in the "Golden Triangle," which consisted of Ballarat, Bendigo and Castlemaine, had no-one to keep order. To try and improve this situation Governor La Trobe recruited many ex-convicts as policemen. This meant that many of them were corrupt.

When the Police raided miners' camps and arrested miners who couldn't buy a Miners Right, there were no jails, so they were chained by the leg to trees and big logs, like animals. Many miners ran off or hid down tunnels they had dug when the cry went out the police or "traps" were coming.

The situation deteriorated until the miners built a stockade and elected Peter Lalor as their leader. These were fairly educated men, all of which could read and write. They felt that there should be no taxation placed on them without representation in Parliament and they demanded changes to the brutal mining laws.

On 30th November the miners burnt their licences and built a stockade. They collected arms to protect themselves. The police attacked on 3rd December, 1854. Twenty-two diggers and five troopers were killed. Peter Lalor, the leader, was shot, but was smuggled out of camp by his friends. Thirteen diggers were captured and tried, but were acquitted.

The Governor was eventually recalled to England and Lalor and the leaders of the revolt were pardoned. Lalor became a Member of Parliament and represented the area. He was not uneducated. He had been to Eton College and had a degree in engineering.

Read the poem.

The Fight at Eureka Stockade

"Was I at Eureka?" His figure was drawn to a youthful height,
And a flood of proud recollections made the fire in his grey eyes bright;
With pleasure they lighted and glisten'd, tho' the digger was grizzled and old,
And we gathered about him and listen'd while the tale of Eureka he told.

"Ah, those were the days,"said the digger, "twas a glorious life that we led,
When fortunes were dug up and lost in a day in the whirl of the years that are dead.
But there's many a veteran now in the land - old knights of the pick and the spade,
Who could tell you in language far stronger than mine 'bout the fight at Eureka Stockade.

"We were all of us young on the diggings in days when the nation had birth -
Light-hearted, and careless, and happy, and the flower of all nations on earth;
But we would have been peaceful an' quiet if the law had but let us alone;
And the fight - let them call it a riot - was due to no fault of our own.

"The creed of our rulers was narrow - they ruled with a merciless hand,
For the mark of the cursed broad arrow was deep in the heart of the land.
They treated us worse than the negroes were treated in slavery's day -
And justice was not for the diggers, as shown by the Bently affray.

"P'r'aps Bently was wrong. If he wasn't the bloodthirsty villain they said,
He was one of the jackals that gather where the carcass of labour is laid.
'Twas b'lieved that he murdered a digger, and they let him off scot-free as well,
And the beacon o' battle was lighted on the night that we burnt his hotel.

"You may talk as you like, but the facts are the same (as you've often been told),
And how could we pay when the licence cost more than the worth of the gold?
We heard in the sunlight the clanking o' chains in the hillocks of clay,
And our mates, they were rounded like cattle an' handcuffed an' driven away.

"The troopers were most of them new-chums, with many a gentleman's son;
And ridin' on horseback was easy, and hunting the diggers was fun.
Why, many poor devils who came from the vessel in rags and down-heeled,
Were copped, if they hadn't their licence, before they set foot on the field.

"But they roused the hot blood that was in us, and the cry came to roll up at last;
And I tell you that something had got to be done when the diggers rolled up in the past.
Yet they say that in spite o' the talkin' it all might have ended in smoke,
But just at the point o' the crisis, the voice of a quiet man spoke.

"We have said all our say and it's useless, you must fight or be slaves!' said the voice;
"If it's fight, and you're wanting a leader, I will lead to the end - take your choice!'
I looked, it was Pete! Peter Lalor! who stood with his face to the skies,
But his figure seemed nobler and taller, and brighter the light of his eyes.

"The blood to his forehead was rushin' as hot as the words from his mouth;
He had come from the wrongs of the old land to see those same wrongs in the South;
The wrongs that had followed our flight from the land where the life of the worker was spoiled.
Still tyranny followed! no wonder the blood of the Irishman boiled.

"And true to his promise, they found him - the mates who are vanished or dead,
Who gathered for justice around him with the flag of the diggers o'erhead.
When the people are cold and unb'lieving, when the hands of the tyrants are strong,
You must sacrifice life for the people before they'll come down on the wrong.

"I'd a mate on the diggings, a lad, curly-headed, an' blue-eyed, an' white,
And the diggers said I was his father, an', well, p'r'aps the diggers were right.

I forbade him to stir from the tent, made him swear on the book he'd obey,
But he followed me in, in the darkness, and - was - shot - on Eureka that day.

"Down, down with the tyrant an' bully,' these were the last words from his mouth
As he caught up a broken pick-handle and struck for the Flag of the South
An' let it in sorrow be written - the worst of this terrible strife,
'Twas under the 'banner of Britain' came the bullet that ended his life.

"I struck then! I struck then for vengeance! When I saw him lie dead in the dirt,
And the blood that came oozing like water had darkened the red of his shirt,
I caught up the weapon he dropped an' I struck with the strength of my hate,
Until I fell wounded an' senseless, half-dead by the side of `my mate'.

"Surprised in the grey o' the morning half-armed, and the Barricade bad,
A battle o' twenty-five minutes was long 'gainst the odds that they had,
But the light o' the morning was deadened an' the smoke drifted far o'er the town
An' the clay o' Eureka was reddened ere the flag o' the diggers came down.

"But it rose in the hands of the people an' high in the breezes it tost,
And our mates only died for a cause that was won by the battle they lost.
When the people are selfish and narrow, when the hands of the tyrants are strong,
You must sacrifice life for the public before they come down on a wrong.

"It is thirty-six years this December - (December the first) since we made
The first stand 'gainst the wrongs of old countries that day in Eureka Stockade,
But the lies and the follies and shams of the North have all landed since then
An' it's pretty near time that you lifted the flag of Eureka again.

"You boast of your progress an' thump empty thunder from out of your drums,
While two of your `marvellous cities' are reeking with alleys an' slums.
An' the landsharks, an' robbers, an' idlers an' -! Yes, I had best draw it mild
But whenever I think o' Eureka my talking is apt to run wild.

"Even now in my tent when I'm dreaming I'll spring from my bunk, strike a light,
And feel for my boots an' revolver, for the diggers' march past in the night.
An' the faces an' forms of old mates an' old comrades go driftin' along,
With a band in the front of 'em playing the tune of an old battle song."

Answer these questions:

1. Do you think the writer of this poem is biased? Explain your answer.

   _____

   _____

   _____

2. Explain what was meant by the following:

   a. flower of all nations on earth: _____

   _____

b. the mark of the cursed broad arrow: _____

_____

c. new-chums: _____

d. the blood to his forehead was rising: _____

_____

e. a cause that was won by the battle they lost: _____

_____

3. Read the poem carefully. Who was Bently? How did the diggers punish
him?

_____

_____

_____

4. Reading the poem, what do you think the author's feelings are about the
Eureka Stockade?

_____

_____

_____

A. Further Work:

Imagine you had run off to the goldfields. Write a story about your adventures and what it was like watching the diggers in the stockade and the fight that ensued.

To be able to do this you will need to do some research on the subject.

B. Definition of poetical terms appear below. Write the name for each description. The first is completed for you.

1. Comparing one thing with another of a different kind   <u>simile</u>

2. Words that imitate the natural sound of things, e.g., buzz _____

3. A figure of speech in which a word or phrase that
    generally means one thing is said to be another, e.g.,
    a sea of glass   _____

4. A play on words, e.g., dreamers often lie   _____

Condensing Sentences

There are two main ways of condensing sentences. One is to omit what is not essential to the main point. The other is to express in fewer words what is essential.

a. **If we know the exact word or the correct technical term we can often make one word do instead of several.**

   For example: Hamlet often speaks aloud his thoughts when no-one else is on stage.

   Better: Hamlet soliloquizes.

b. **If the items of a list belong to one class of things, the class name will serve for them all.**

   For example: Mrs Jones soaked her tea-towels, pillowcases, and table-cloths before washing them.

   Better: Mrs Jones soaked her linen before washing them.

c. **We may omit any word that merely repeats the sense of another.**

   For example: One of the two halves of the lemon was put away in the fridge.

   Better: One half of the lemon was put in the fridge.

d. **Often a single word may be found to express the meaning of a phrase.**

   For example: After an interval of several minutes he returned.

   Better: Presently he returned.

e. **A single word can also be used to replace a clause.**

   For example: We have done what is expected of us.

   Better: We have done our duty.

f. **If a single word can not be used to replace a clause, sometimes a phrase can.**

   For example: That he managed to keep his temper in those circumstances is a great achievement.

   Better: To keep his temper in those circumstances is a great achievement.

g. **Sometimes a whole sentence may be shortened to a word or phrase.**

   For example: The sun was just going down. Our friends arrived. They were on horseback.

   Better: At sunset our friends arrived mounted.

h. **Occasionally we can save words by finding an entirely different way of expressing things.**

For example: I had already posted my letter when I received yours.

Better: Our letters crossed.

i. **Sometimes we are long winded or pompous.**

For example: the financially underprivileged   or   in the vicinity

Better: the poor   nearby

Condense and rewrite each of these sentences to the number of words indicated in brackets.

1. Past history suggests we never learn from the mistakes in history. (6)
   _____

2. The weather is unexpected considering the season. (4)
   _____

3. He spoke with mild anger. (3)
   _____

4. When the first sight of morning light appears he starts work. He does this every day of his life. (6)
   _____

5. Always answer your letters by return of post. (4)
   _____

6. The old man looked as happy as a hungry schoolboy in a well stocked pantry. (6)
   _____

7. It was strange for a lawyer to die without a will. (6)
   _____

8. In the twinkling of an eye he achieved what he was aiming for. (5)
   _____

9. I know what all these figures add up to. I know this with a certainty. (6)
   _____

Napoleon's Early Years

Napoleon was born in Corsica in 1769 A.D. His family was noble, although not wealthy. France acquired Corsica from Genoa, Italy, in the year of his birth.

He was educated in mainland France and went on to graduate from a military academy in 1785. He then became a second lieutenant in an artillery regiment of the French Army.

The French Revolution began in 1789. Within three years the monarchy had been overthrown and a French republic proclaimed. During the early years of the revolution Napoleon was at home in Corsica, where he became affiliated with a pro-democracy political group, the Jacobins. He returned to his military duties in 1793 when he and his family were forced, due to a disagreement with the Corsican Governor, to flee to mainland France.

In France Napoleon became associated with Robespierre, a Jacobin who was a key force behind the Reign of Terror. During this time he was promoted to the rank of brigadier general. When Robespierre fell from power he was under house arrest for a time, but he helped suppress a royalist insurrection against the military government and was promoted to major general.

The following year, the Directory, the five person group that had governed France since 1795, offered to let Napoleon lead an invasion of England. Napoleon decided that France's naval forces were not yet ready to attack the superior British Royal Navy. Instead he proposed an invasion of Egypt in an effort to wipe out British trade routes with India. His troops won a victory against Egypt's military rulers, the Mamluks, at the Battle of the Pyramids in July 1798. However his forces were stranded after his naval fleet was decimated by the British at the Battle of the Nile in August 1798.

Despite this in early 1799, Napoleon's army launched an invasion of Ottoman-ruled Syria, which ended with the failed siege of Acre, a town in modern day Israel. With the political situation in France so uncertain, Napoleon opted to abandon his army in Egypt and return to France, where in the same year, he was part of a group that successfully overthrew the French Directory.

The Directory was replaced by a three-member Consulate, and Napoleon became the first Consul and the leading political figure. This power was cemented in June 1800, at the Battle of Marengo, when Napoleon defeated one of France's main enemies, Austria. He also made peace with Britain at the Treaty of Amiens in 1802, although this peace only lasted a year.

Napoleon was then able to restore stability to France. He centralised the government; instituted reforms such as banking and education; supported science and the arts; and sought to improve relations between his regime and the Pope, who represented France's main religion, Catholicism, which had suffered during the revolution. His most significant accomplishment was the Napoleonic Code that streamlined the legal system and formed the foundation of modern French law.

A. Answer these questions:

1. From the text explain why you think the years 1769 –1793 were important in setting Napoleon on the road to First Consul, and later Emperor.

_____

_____

_____

2. What reason did Napoleon give for declining to invade England?

_____

_____

3. What did Napoleon propose as a better alternative? Why?

_____

_____

4. Did Napoleon succeed ? Answer in detail.

_____

_____

5. In which direction did Napoleon turn next? Did he succeed?

_____

6. Why did Napoleon return to France? Was this a wise decision?

_____

_____

7. List Napoleon's attempts to restore stability to France once peace was achieved.

_____

_____

8. Research and write several paragraphs about the Napoleonic Code.

B. Word Knowledge: choose a word from the text that means the same as each definition below.

1. an act of rebellion _____

2. destroyed a great number of _____

3. bound or united _____

4. being in close of association with _____

Australian Poetry Through the Ages: Banjo Patterson

Andrew Barton Paterson, known to people as Banjo Paterson, along with Henry Lawson, is considered one of Australia's best known poets. His family owned a race horse named Banjo and in his earlier writings for the *Bulletin*, Paterson used the pseudonym 'The Banjo'.

Banjo Paterson was born at Narambla Station, New South Wales in 1864 but considered his home on Illalong Station near Yass, New South Wales as his child-hood home. Many experiences during his childhood, where he was in contact with drovers, bushrangers, and teamsters became the basis for his writings

His first published poem was *El Mahdi to the Australian Troops.* He was only 21 years old when it was published by *the Bulletin* in February 1885. Two of his best known poems are "*The Man From Snowy River*" and "*Clancy of the Overflow.*"

"*The Man from Snowy River*" tells the story of a valuable horse which escapes and the vast sum offered by its owner for its safe return. All the riders in the area gather to pursue the wild bush horses and cut the valuable horse from the mob. But the country defeats them all, except for the 'Man from Snowy River'. His personal courage and skill has turned him into a legend.

There is disagreement as to whether Banjo Patterson based the character of the Man from Snowy River on Jack Riley of Corryong or if he was a composite character from a number of people he met.

Read the poem below carefully. It is a very long poem but has been presented in its entirety to allow you to experience the full effect of it. Try and visualize it as you read.

The Man from Snowy River

There was movement at the station, for the word had passed around
That the colt from old Regret had got away,
And had joined the wild bush horses - he was worth a thousand pound,
So all the cracks had gathered to the fray.
All the tried and noted riders from the stations near and far
Had mustered at the homestead overnight,
For the bushmen love hard riding where the wild bush horses are,
And the stockhorse snuffs the battle with delight.

There was Harrison, who made his pile when Pardon won the cup,
The old man with his hair as white as snow;
But few could ride beside him when his blood was fairly up -
He would go wherever horse and man could go.
And Clancy of the Overflow came down to lend a hand,
No better horseman ever held the reins;
For never horse could throw him while the saddle girths would stand,
He learnt to ride while droving on the plains.

And one was there, a stripling on a small and weedy beast,
He was something like a racehorse undersized,
With a touch of Timor pony - three parts thoroughbred at least -
And such as are by mountain horsemen prized.
He was hard and tough and wiry - just the sort that won't say die -
There was courage in his quick impatient tread;
And he bore the badge of gameness in his bright and fiery eye,
And the proud and lofty carriage of his head.

But still so slight and weedy, one would doubt his power to stay,
And the old man said, "That horse will never do
For a long a tiring gallop - lad, you'd better stop away,
Those hills are far too rough for such as you."
So he waited sad and wistful - only Clancy stood his friend -
"I think we ought to let him come," he said;
"I warrant he'll be with us when he's wanted at the end,
For both his horse and he are mountain bred".

"He hails from Snowy River, up by Kosciusko's side,
Where the hills are twice as steep and twice as rough,
Where a horse's hoofs strike firelight from the flint stones every stride,
The man that holds his own is good enough.
And the Snowy River riders on the mountains make their home,
Where the river runs those giant hills between;
I have seen full many horsemen since I first commenced to roam,
But nowhere yet such horsemen have I seen."

So he went - they found the horses by the big mimosa clump -
They raced away towards the mountain's brow,
And the old man gave his orders, "Boys, go at them from the jump,
No use to try for fancy riding now.
And, Clancy, you must wheel them, try and wheel them to the right.
Ride boldly, lad, and never fear the spills,
For never yet was rider that could keep the mob in sight,
If once they gain the shelter of those hills."

So Clancy rode to wheel them - he was racing on the wing
Where the best and boldest riders take their place,
And he raced his stockhorse past them, and he made the ranges ring
With the stockwhip, as he met them face to face.
Then they halted for a moment, while he swung the dreaded lash,
But they saw their well-loved mountain full in view,
And they charged beneath the stockwhip with a sharp and sudden dash,
And off into the mountain scrub they flew.

Then fast the horsemen followed, where the gorges deep and black
Resounded to the thunder of their tread,
And the stockwhips woke the echoes, and they fiercely answered back
From cliffs and crags that beetled overhead.
And upward, ever upward, the wild horses held their way,
Where mountain ash and kurrajong grew wide;
And the old man muttered fiercely, "We may bid the mob good day,
No man can hold them down the other side."

Australian Homeschooling #563
Successful English 8B

When they reached the mountain's summit, even Clancy took a pull,
It well might make the boldest hold their breath,
The wild hop scrub grew thickly, and the hidden ground was full
Of wombat holes, and any slip was death.
But the man from Snowy River let the pony have his head,
And he swung his stockwhip round and gave a cheer,
And he raced him down the mountain like a torrent down its bed,
While the others stood and watched in very fear.

He sent the flint stones flying, but the pony kept his feet,
He cleared the fallen timber in his stride,
And the man from Snowy River never shifted in his seat -
It was grand to see that mountain horseman ride.
Through the stringybarks and saplings, on the rough and broken ground,
Down the hillside at a racing pace he went;
And he never drew the bridle till he landed safe and sound,
At the bottom of that terrible descent.

He was right among the horses as they climbed the further hill,
And the watchers on the mountain standing mute,
Saw him ply the stockwhip fiercely, he was right among them still,
As he raced across the clearing in pursuit.
Then they lost him for a moment, where two mountain gullies met
In the ranges, but a final glimpse reveals
On a dim and distant hillside the wild horses racing yet,
With the man from Snowy River at their heels.

And he ran them single-handed till their sides were white with foam.
He followed like a bloodhound on their track,
Till they halted cowed and beaten, then he turned their heads for home,
And alone and unassisted brought them back.
But his hardy mountain pony he could scarcely raise a trot,
He was blood from hip to shoulder from the spur;
But his pluck was still undaunted, and his courage fiery hot,
For never yet was mountain horse a cur.

And down by Kosciusko, where the pine-clad ridges raise
Their torn and rugged battlements on high,
Where the air is clear as crystal, and the white stars fairly blaze
At midnight in the cold and frosty sky,
And where around The Overflow the reed beds sweep and sway
To the breezes, and the rolling plains are wide,
The man from Snowy River is a household word today,
And the stockmen tell the story of his ride.

Answer the questions:

1. The poem is full of vivid imagery. Give three examples from **throughout** the poem. Explain their impact.

_____

_____

_____

_____

_____

_____

2. The pace of the poem is fast due to its theme. Give 4 examples of words that help the reader understand the speed of the chase.

   _____

   _____

3. The poem also contains vivid descriptions of countryside. Give 4 examples and explain how these help give depth to the poem.

   _____

   _____

   _____

   _____

4. What type of form has been used?

   _____

5. Describe the tone of the poem. (The poet's subjective views and attitudes.

   _____

   _____

   _____

6. Poetry is meant to be enjoyed. Explain what you liked about this poem.

   _____

   _____

Further Work:

It is impossible to cover all the poems written by Banjo Patterson in this book. You will therefore need to do further reading for yourself.

Read "Clancy of the Overflow."

Write an essay analysing the poem. Include the following:

- theme
- form
- diction (word choice)

- tone
- imagery
- rhyme

Types of Sentences

Sentences may be classified according to their grammatical structure.

- **The <u>simple sentence,</u> which contains only one clause.**
  For example: One summer afternoon we went to the beach.

- **The <u>compound sentence,</u> which contains two or more principal clauses.**
  For example: She soon gave up playing and went to the window.

- **The complex sentence, which consists of a principal clause and one or more subordinate clauses.**
  For example: She stared out into the sunbaked garden, which was empty now and very still.

We learn grammar so we can understand how sentences are built.

A. Complete each simple sentence below by rewriting to add a missing subject or predicate. The first one is completed for you.

1. .... my new pair of shoes?
    <u>Do you like my new pair of shoes?</u>

2. Into the middle of the room was suddenly flung.............

    _____

3. The boy ....

    _____

4. Where did you put ....?

    _____

B. Combine each group of sentences into a single <u>compound</u> or <u>complex</u> sentence.

1. We prefer wool. It makes the best suits.

    _____

2. I was driving along Smith Street. I was hailed by a man.

    _____

3. It was last year. Mary Jones went to Japan.

    _____

4. The sheriff shot the bandits. You met him in the canyon today.

    _____

A. By now the majority of your sentences should be complex sentences. Simple sentences should only be used to create an effect. Combining two sentences with a conjunction is a easy way of turning simple sentences into complex sentences.

Rewrite the two simple sentences as a complex sentence using a conjunction to join them. Use a different conjunction each time.

1. He opened his book. He read a chapter.

   _____

2. Nearly a month passed. I received your email.

   _____

3. I can not buy a bicycle. I have saved more money.

   _____

4. Andrew did not pass his exams. He did not study.

   _____

5. They arrived. I was still eating my breakfast.

   _____

B. Build a complex sentence by adding phrases or clauses.

1. I should never have believed........

   _____

2. ....he could just see over the top.

   _____

3. He asked if anyone would mind.............

   _____

4. I have never quite understood...............

   _____

5. Though I tried very hard............

   _____

6. The tractor..................broke down on the way to the paddock.

   _____

7. ....(adverbial of time) I discovered the tennis ball..................

   _____

Napoleonic Wars

On May 18th, 1804 Napoleon proclaimed himself Emperor and crowned himself, on December 2nd, 1804. In 1808 he began to recreate an aristocracy, a tradition that had been eliminated by the Revolution, by granting titles to people who served him particularly well. His court became a place of pomp and elegance with protocol and rules of etiquette that were very regimented. His wife, Josephine, loved the court but, despite the fact that Napoleon created it, he was uncomfortable there and worked long hours to escape it.

By 1805 Napoleon had his forces massed on the French coast of the English Channel preparing for an amphibious assault. The Channel was heavily defended by the British fleet under Nelson, however, if the French managed to land in Britain, the British did not have a large enough army to defend the island.

The Russian and Austrian army, seeing their chance, marched on France and Napoleon was forced to divert his army to handle the threat, though he continued to put naval pressure on England. On October 21st, 1805, the British fleet decimated Napoleon's fleet at the Battle of Trafalgar, thus solidifying their naval supremacy.

Napoleon smashed the Russo-Austrian offensive in Moravia at Austerlitz, on December 2nd, 1805, thus solidifying his hold on Europe. The Russians retreated to Poland and the Austrians signed the Treaty of Pressburg, which seceded even more Austrian territory to Napoleon.

Next Napoleon dissolved the Holy Roman Empire replacing it with the Confederation of the Rhine. He defeated Prussia at the battles of Jena and Auerstadt in October 1806. Napoleon now controlled western Prussia, including Berlin.

Afterwards he pursued Russia, overrunning their army at Friedland on June 14th, 1807. Alexander was afraid of retreating into Russia in case a rebellion broke out when fighting started on Russian soil, so he negotiated the Treaty of Tilsit with Napoleon in July 1807, and became his ally. To get this treaty Napoleon appealed to Alexander's ego, claiming they were alike and, while Napoleon's destiny was a European empire, Alexander would be Emperor of the East, ruling Turkey and India. He also claimed that Alexander's problems were caused by England.

After his navy was destroyed at Trafalgar in 1805, Napoleon realised that if his empire was to be secure he must defeat England. Since he could not beat the navy he decided to wage economic warfare against them. His plan, known as the Continental System, begun in 1806, was to restrict England from entering and trading with Europe. Napoleon demanded his empire close their ports to British goods and he got the Russians, Austrians and Prussians to co-operate with his plan. He hoped that without having the European markets to buy their manufactured products Britain would have a severe depression which would prevent them from maintaining their navy and give France a chance to build its own manufacturing industries. England retaliated by creating a blockade of European ships anywhere on the oceans controlled by England.

Australian Poetry Through the Ages: Banjo Paterson 2

Paterson led a very interesting life. His interests included being a crocodile hunter, pearl diver, and amateur sportsman. His interests in politics led him to leave his law studies and become a war correspondent where he covered the Boer War and the Chinese Boxer Rebellion. He continued to travel the world learning first hand about politics.

Then while touring Australia in 1902, Paterson met Alice Emily Walker at Tenterfield Station in northern New South Wales. He married her at the station on April 8, 1903. They made their home in Woollahra, a suburb of Sydney after he was appointed editor of the *Sydney Evening News.*

In 1914 Paterson left for England to become a war correspondent during the First World War. Unable to secure a position, he became an ambulance driver instead. He returned to Australia where he enlisted and was commissioned as a lieutenant in the A.I.F. He spent his war years in the Middle East and rose to the rank of Major. Alice joined her husband in 1917 and worked for two years as a volunteer at the hospital in Ismailia. In 1919 the two returned to Australia where he went back to writing. He wrote for *Smith's Weekly,* edited the *Sydney Sportsman* along with a variety of fiction, verse and radio scripts.

In 1930 Paterson retired from journalism. He died on February 5, 1941.

Banjo was known not only for the song "Waltzing Matilda," but also for his attempt to improve the lives of his fellow Australians by exposing their hardships to the public.

The following two poems illustrate his love for Australia and its animals. Read them and answer the questions.

Old Man Platypus

Far from the trouble and toil of town,
Where the reed beds sweep and shiver,
Look at a fragment of velvet brown–
Old Man Platypus drifting down,
Drifting along the river.
And he plays and dives in the river bends
In a style that is most elusive;
With few relations and fewer friends,
For Old Man Platypus descends
From a family most exclusive.
He shares his burrow beneath the bank
With his wife and his son and daughter
At the roots of the reeds and the grasses rank;
And the bubbles show where our hero sank
To its entrance under water.
Safe in their burrow below the falls
They live in a world of wonder,

A. Word Knowledge: choose a word from the text that means the same as each definition below.

1. cause something to change course or turn from one direction to another _____

2. military forces by both land and sea _____

3. to withdraw formally from an alliance _____

4. uniting firmly or consolidating _____

5. completely remove or get rid of _____

B. Answer these questions:

1. Where was Napoleon planning to attack in 1805? What would have been the result if he had managed to land in England?

    _____

    _____

    _____

2. What diverted Napoleon from his plan?

    _____

    _____

3. Name the naval battle and date it occurred where Napoleon's fleet was totally defeated.

    _____

4. Which countries did Napoleon defeat between December 1805 and June 1807?

    _____

    _____

5. Since Napoleon could not defeat England on the sea what other measures did he take to try and defeat them?

    _____

    _____

6. What did the British do in return?

    _____

C. The Battle of Trafalgar was an important naval battle. Find out more about it and write at least 3 paragraphs outlining what you found.

Where no one visits and no one calls,
They sleep like little brown billiard balls
With their beaks tucked neatly under.
And he talks in a deep unfriendly growl
As he goes on his journey lonely;
For he's no relation to fish nor fowl,
Nor to bird nor beast, nor to horned owl;
In fact, he's the one and only!

Answer the questions:

1. What type of form has been used?

   _____

2. Outline the theme of the poem.

   _____

   _____

3. Outline some of the words Paterson has used to convey movement.

   _____

   _____

4. Discuss some of the other imagery used in this poem.

   _____

   _____

   _____

5. This poem is different to many of his other poems. State whether or not you enjoyed the poem. Explain your answer.

   _____

   _____

By the Grey Gulf Water

Far to the Northward there lies a land,
A wonderful land that the winds blow over,
And none may fathom nor understand
The charm it holds for the restless rover;
A great grey chaos -- a land half made,
Where endless space is and no life stirreth;
And the soul of a man will recoil afraid
From the sphinx-like visage that Nature weareth.
But old Dame Nature, though scornful, craves
Her dole of death and her share of slaughter;
Many indeed are the nameless graves
Where her victims sleep by the Grey Gulf-water.

Slowly and slowly those grey streams glide,
Drifting along with a languid motion,
Lapping the reed-beds on either side,
Wending their way to the Northern Ocean.
Grey are the plains where the emus pass
Silent and slow, with their staid demeanour;
Over the dead men's graves the grass
Maybe is waving a trifle greener.
Down in the world where men toil and spin
Dame Nature smiles as man's hand has taught her;
Only the dead men her smiles can win
In the great lone land by the Grey Gulf-water.

For the strength of man is an insect's strength
In the face of that mighty plain and river,
And the life of a man is a moment's length
To the life of the stream that will run for ever.
And so it cometh they take no part
In small-world worries; each hardy rover
Rideth abroad and is light of heart,
With the plains around and the blue sky over.
And up in the heavens the brown lark sings
The songs that the strange wild land has taught her;
Full of thanksgiving her sweet song rings --
And I wish I were back by the Grey Gulf-water.

It is not clear exactly what place Paterson is writing about but it was obviously somewhere in the north of Australia, possibly the Gulf of Carpentaria.

Answer these questions:

1. What is the theme of this poem?

_____

_____

2. This poem is full of vivid images. Outline some of them.

_____

_____

_____

_____

3. Personification has been used in this poem. State who and what has been personified. Is it effective? Explain why you think so.

_____

_____

_____

4. Man has been compared to Nature. State how man has been described. How has this added to our insight into the land?

_____

_____

_____

_____

5. You have now looked at quite a number of poems by Patterson. State which you liked best and explain why.

_____

_____

_____

_____

Paterson wrote other nature poems. These include:
- **Sunrise On the Coast**
- **At the Melting of the Snow**
- **Black Swans**
- **The Daylight is Dying**

Find, read and enjoy them.

Correct Word

Choose from the box the adjective that means:

> vindictive, pensive, contemptuous, irascible, auxiliary, rotary, ponderous, aquatic

1. taking place on the water   _____

2. quick tempered, irritable   _____

3. moving round like a wheel   _____

4. having a great desire for revenge   _____

5. expressing deep hatred or disapproval   _____

6. weighty or slow owing to weight   _____

7. providing supplementary or additional help   _____

8. engaged in deep or serious thought   _____

Word Meanings

Choose a word from the box to fit each meaning below:

monotonous, enumerate, scrupulous, avaricious, symptom, obscure, militant, contagious, garrulous, biennial, parapet, consequence, profile, complacent, inaudible, calamity, intangible, infectious, lament,

1. side view of the head   _____

2. talkative   _____

3. breast high wall to protect people   _____

4. a great misfortune   _____

5. happening once or twice a year   _____

6. having an extreme greed for material gain   _____

7. to mourn or make cries of grief   _____

8. favouring confrontational or violent methods
    in support of a cause   _____

9. showing uncritical satisfaction with oneself   _____

10. that which indicates the existence of
    something else   _____

11. to count the number of or to name over   _____

12. able to spread and infect another   _____

13. a cause or effect, typically one that is
    unpleasant   _____

14. dull, tedious and repetitious   _____

15. unable to be heard   _____

16. not easily discovered or known about   _____

17. not made of a physical substance, not able
    to be touched   _____

18, thorough and extremely attentive to detail   _____

Learn the words you do not know.

More Complex Sentences

A. Add an adverbial clause or phrase.

1. ....I will bath the dog. (adverbial phrase starting with after)

   _____

2. He ran so hard .... (clause starting with that)

   _____

3. This week he is bowling better ..... (clause beginning with than)

   _____

4. ....we enjoyed ourselves immensely. (phrase beginning with In spite of)

   _____

5. Mr Brown is not so old............ (clause beginning with as)

   _____

6. .... we found a large snake. (phrase beginning with under)

   _____

B. Add adjectival clauses to complete the sentences.

1. The child who crosses the road without looking.................

   _____

2. An instrument .... is called a microscope.

   _____

3. Friends, who help you in time of need...............

   _____

4. The person.................... may find his way anywhere.

   _____

5. A person .... is known as a psychologist.

   _____

6. .... you don't want is dear at any price.

   _____

© Valerie Marett
Coroneos Publications

Australian Homeschooling #563
Successful English 8B

Napoleonic Empire

Napoleon came very close to including most of Europe into the blockade against England. By the 1807 Treaty of Tilsit, Russia and Prussia agreed to co-operate and these countries and Austria declared war on Britain. Napoleon also tried to force Denmark and Portugal to join the blockade. Since Denmark contained ports crucial to English trade, the English navy blockaded Copenhagen and attacked the Danish fleet in hopes of keeping the port open. Instead it made the Danes willing to co-operate with Napoleon.

The Continental System ended up hurting Napoleon more than Britain. It slowed the internal European economy and tariffs on goods going into France, but not goods coming out of France, damaging the economies of Europe further. It did cause a rise in manufacturing in France, but led to resentment in the other countries. Since land transport was slow, Eastern Europe had major problems obtaining goods from Western Europe.

The Continental System led to the Peninsula War, which sapped French strength, morale and prestige. In the end France was damaged but not Britain, as Britain compensated for the loss of continental trade by stepping up trade with its colonies.

Between 1809 and 1811, Napoleon's Empire stood at its greatest extent. However, Napoleon became worried he had no heir, so he divorced Josephine and married Marie Louise of Austria, who in 1811 gave birth to a son.

By 1811 Napoleon's Empire included nearly all of Europe except for the Balkans. It was comprised of France, which had swallowed up Belgium, Holland, parts of Germany and the Italian coast all the way to Rome. Napoleon held alliances with Austria, Russia, Denmark, Sweden and Prussia. Almost all of Europe was now at war with Britain, their resources, industry and population being used to serve the French Empire. All of these states participated in the Continental System.

Napoleon made use of his large family, appointing his brothers and sisters as royalty throughout Europe. With Napoleon now related to most of Europe, he reintroduced the nobility and within two decades of the French Revolution a new aristocracy came into existence.

Although he granted nobility, his dominance of the European continent continued to spread the liberal ideas of the French Revolution. He spread the Napoleonic Code to all of the territories he controlled with only minor changes from place to place. He also spread the idea that all citizens were equal before the law and that legal privileges for certain classes did not exist. He did what he could to end the feudal peasantry, although it seemed to continue even though it was outlawed. This was because the same people owned land and the same people continued to work it. Napoleon also spread the metric system.

Napoleon, and many of the French, saw the Napoleonic Empire as a recreation of the Roman Empire. Across Europe he constructed Triumphal Arches in the style of the Romans and it appeared, for a while at least, that his dream of a unified Europe was a distinct possibility.

A. Answer these questions:

1. Explain the idea behind the Continental System.

   _____

   _____

2. Did the Continental System achieve its aim? Explain your answer.

   _____

   _____

   _____

3. What countries were included in the Napoleonic Empire by 1811?

   _____

   _____

   _____

4. Explain how, despite granting nobility to his family and some followers, Napoleon spread the ideas of the French Revolution.

   _____

   _____

5. What Empire did Napoleon imagine his Empire was a recreation of?

   _____

6. England turned to her colonies to supply her needs. What did Australia contribute in 1811? (If you don't know you need to research.)

   _____

   _____

B. Word Knowledge. Find a word that means the following:

1. the confidence, definition and enthusiasm of a group at a particular time   _____

2. critical in the success of something   _____

3. a system of rules   _____

C. Research and write:

The Industrial Revolution occurred about this time. Give a summary of some of the ways this affected England.

Australian Poetry Through the Ages: Women Poets

Dorothea Mackellar was a third generation Australian who loved Australia and the Australian countryside. She is best remembered for her poem, "My Country", which you will find below. In the 1950's and 1960's every Australian primary school child memorised this poem.

This poem expresses Dorothea Mackellar's deep passion and love for her country, Australia. She describes it as beautiful land: a land of contrasts.

My Country

The love of field and coppice,
Of green and shaded lanes.
Of ordered woods and gardens
Is running in your veins,
Strong love of grey-blue distance
Brown streams and soft dim skies
I know but cannot share it,
My love is otherwise.

I love a sunburnt country,
A land of sweeping plains,
Of ragged mountain ranges,
Of droughts and flooding rains.
I love her far horizons,
I love her jewel-sea,
Her beauty and her terror -
The wide brown land for me!

A stark white ring-barked forest
All tragic to the moon,
The sapphire-misted mountains,
The hot gold hush of noon.
Green tangle of the brushes,
Where lithe lianas coil,
And orchids deck the tree-tops
And ferns the warm dark soil.

Core of my heart, my country!
Her pitiless blue sky,
When sick at heart, around us,
We see the cattle die -
But then the grey clouds gather,
And we can bless again
The drumming of an army,
The steady, soaking rain.

Core of my heart, my country!
Land of the Rainbow Gold,
For flood and fire and famine,

She pays us back threefold -
Over the thirsty paddocks,
Watch, after many days,
The filmy veil of greenness
That thickens as we gaze.

An opal-hearted country,
A wilful, lavish land -
All you who have not loved her,
You will not understand -
Though earth holds many splendours,
Wherever I may die,
I know to what brown country
My homing thoughts will fly.

A. Answer these questions:

1. Dorothea Mackellar has entitled this poem "My Country." What country is she referring to?

   _____

2. The first verse opens with talk of another country she knows. Which country is she speaking of?

   _____

3. Dorothea Mackellar has used phrases and lines that are opposite to provide a contrast, e.g., "her beauty and her terror." Give 3 further examples.

   _____

   _____

4. Discuss the contrast between the country mentioned in the first verse and Australia as mentioned in the second verse.

   _____

   _____

   _____

5. Give examples from the poem of the following poetic devices and what they inspire in the reader:

   a. onomatopoeia: _____

   _____

   b. personification: _____

   _____

© Valerie Marett
Coroneos Publications

Australian Homeschooling #563
Successful English 8B

c.   alliteration: _____

_____

6. Dorothea Mackellar uses a variety of phrases to describe Australia from its mountain ranges to the sea. All of her imagery is vivid. List some of these.

_____

_____

_____

_____

7. It has been said that the poet was in love with the Australian landscape and evoked the same feeling in her readers. Do you think this holds true for Australians today? Explain your answer.

_____

_____

_____

_____

_____

The "Song of Australia" was the result of a competition sponsored by the Gawler Institute in South Australia in 1859 to celebrate its second anniversary. There were 96 entries but it was the five verse song, written by English-born poet, Caroline J. Carleton which was awarded the first prize of ten guineas. Until "Advance Australia Fair" became the national anthem "Song of Australia was sung in most South Australian schools and at many state events after "God Save the Queen."

Note the differences between this poem and the previous one, although both clearly loved Australia. N.B. The words 'witching harmonies' is a shortened form of bewitching harmonies.

The Song of Australia

There is a land where summer skies
Are gleaming with a thousand dyes,
Blending in witching harmonies, in harmonies;
And grassy knoll, and forest height,
Are flushing in the rosy light,
And all above is azure bright -
Australia!

There is a land where honey flows,
Where laughing corn luxuriant grows,
Land of the myrtle and the rose,
On hill and plain the clust'ring vine,

Is gushing out with purple wine,
And cups are quaffed to thee and thine -
Australia!

There is a land where treasures shine
Deep in the dark unfathomed mine,
For worshippers at Mammon's shrine,
Where gold lies hid, and rubies gleam,
And fabled wealth no more doth seem
The idle fancy of a dream -
Australia!

There is a land where homesteads peep
From sunny plain and woodland steep,
And love and joy bright vigils keep,
Where the glad voice of childish glee
Is mingling with the melody
Of nature's hidden minstrelsy -
Australia!

There is a land where, floating free,
From mountain top to girdling sea,
A proud flag waves exultingly,
And freedom's sons the banner bear,
No shackled slave can breathe the air,
Fairest of Britain's daughters fair -
Australia!

Answer these questions:

1. Give examples of the way Caroline Carleton has contrasted different aspects of Australia.

   _____

   _____

   _____

2. Explain the following:

   a. azure bright: _____

   b. quaffed: _____

   c. Mammon's shrine: _____

3. Both "My Country" and "The Song of Australia" portray the love of Australia but they are very different. Explain at least one main difference.

   _____

   _____

   _____

4. Find 2 examples of alliteration in the poem.

_____

5. What is the effect of repeating the word "Australia" at the end of each verse?

_____

_____

6. What is the tone of the poem?

_____

_____

Further Work:

We are fortunate to live in a vast and beautiful land. Write an essay or poem showing your patriotism and describing how you feel about Australia.

Indirect Speech

Change the following into indirect speech.

1. "Oh dear, I have broken another glass," said Mrs Robinson in dismay.

_____

2. "Put that vase down at once!" said Father to his small son.

_____

3. "How brilliant the stars are tonight," said Stella.

_____

4. "Hi Tony! Nice morning!" called Robert. "How are you doing today?"

_____

5. "Get out of here! Now!" snapped the guard.

_____

6. "Do buy me one, Mummy!" begged Margaret.

_____

7. "I really liked their music," said James. "I think that is the best song they have ever sung."

Colons

Colons indicate a division in writing—a pause in speech—greater than that of a comma and less than that of a full stop. It usually separates a general, introductory item from a specific explanation, list, quotation, number or the like. It has four principal uses:

- **the salutation of a formal speech or report,**
  e.g., Mr President, Committee Members and Distinguished Guests, To Whom it May Concern.

- **after a word, phrase or statement that introduces a list or an item,**
  e.g., Groceries for tomorrow: milk, bread, cheese, oranges, meat.

- **after a statement that introduces a quotation, another statement or an explanation or amplification of what has just been said,**
  e.g., My conclusions is: cats are the most beautiful of all animals.

- **to separate the hour from the minutes in a numerical writing of the time; or the volume number from the page number in a citation from a publication,**
  e.g., Psalm 55:4

Rewrite the sentences using a colon correctly.

1. I wish I had a job. I am a great worker and need the money.

   _____

2. I have three objections to the plan. It would take too long, cost too much and be too dangerous.

   _____

   _____

3. The friends I play with are Jill, Jack, Tom and Eden.

   _____

4. Wayne excels in the following sports, cricket, basketball and rowing.

   _____

5. My alarm clock is set for six forty five a.m.

   _____

6. You will need the following back to school items, pencils, erasers and markers.

   _____

   _____

Napoleon's Downfall

On December 31st, 1810 Czar Alexander 1 withdrew Russia from the Continental System and began trading openly with England. Napoleon was incensed and soon sent his massive Grand Army, comprised of 60,000 soldiers from all the nations he dominated to Poland, ready to force a decisive victory with the Czar's army. He expected Russia to attack his armies but this did not happen. Napoleon then moved his army into Russia in June 1812. The Russians retreated, burning and destroying the countryside they left behind.

Finally, in September 1812, Napoleon confronted the Russian army and won a victory. He entered Moscow, which had been ruined under the Russian scorched-earth policy. The Russian winter that year started unusually early and proved to be particularly harsh. Lacking food and adequate shelter, Napoleon tried to negotiate with Alexander, who refused. This forced Napoleon to retreat but the Russian winter, and lack of supplies decimated the Grand Army and Napoleon emerged with only a few of the soldiers he took in.

Sensing trouble as a result of his failure he left his shattered army and quickly raised a new army, which was not as well trained as the veterans of the Grand Army. He was correct about the trouble, as in 1813 Austria and Prussia joined Alexander along with many German patriots of the Rhine. Meanwhile in June, the Duke of Wellington, leading English troops, fought the coalition at Leipzig. Napoleon lost.

After much negotiating, on April 4th, 1814, Napoleon finally abdicated under the Treaty of Fontainebleau. Talleyrand suggested Louis XVIII as the new king of France and his suggestion was accepted. Louis had the good sense not to try and return France to the old ways before the Revolution. He accepted a "Constitutional Charter" allowing equality and equal access to all government jobs and he kept the Napoleonic Code and several other reforms.

On May 30th, 1814, Louis XVIII signed the Treaty of Paris. This restricted France to its 1792 boundaries. Napoleon was exiled to Elba, a Mediterranean island in Tuscany.

Although Napoleon's Continental System was a disastrous failure during this time, he was undoubtedly the dominant force in Europe. However French dominance inspired local nationalism in Germany and Spain and brought his rule to an end.

The Russian handling of Napoleon's onslaught was very skilful. Instead of fighting, the scorched earth policy, in which everything left behind was burnt, was utilised and seriously hurt Napoleon as he did not generally supply his army but allowed it to live off the land it occupied. Starving and cold, the Grand Army marched into Russia and this ultimately resulted in ruin.

At the same time England was fighting with France, it was also fighting with the United States. Napoleon agreed to lift the Continental System of trade and trade with the United States if they did not trade with Britain and this led to Britain retaliating with the War of 1812. The war ended with a stand-off, effectively establishing the United States sovereignty.

A. Word Knowledge. Find a word that means the following:

1. faced, met, challenged   _____

2. striking back, extracting retribution   _____

3. enraged, infuriated   _____

4. relinquished, renounced   _____

5. taken advantage of   _____

B. Answer these questions:

1. What precipitated Napoleon's invasion of Russia?

_____

_____

_____

2. Explain Russia's strategy for defeating Napoleon and why it worked.

_____

_____

_____

_____

_____

3. What other factors caused Napoleon's defeat in Russia?

_____

_____

_____

4. The best soldiers in Napoleon's Army died in Russia. What did he do to rectify the situation? How did this loss affect his future campaigns?

_____

_____

5. When did Napoleon finally abdicate? Who was the next leader of France?

_____

_____

6. A similar system to Napoleon's Continental System is in force today. What is it? Is it working any better? Discuss this with an adult.

Australian Poetry Through the Ages: Other Poets

Frank Hudson lived from 1913-1988. He was a poet, short story writer and teacher. Read the poem carefully and listen to the nostalgia for the early days of Australia and the hope that the pioneering spirit is not lost.

Pioneers

We are the Old-world people,
Ours were the hearts to dare;
But our youth is spent, and our backs are bent,
And the snow is in our hair.

Back in the early fifties,
Dim through the mists of years,
By the bush-grown strand of a wild, strange land,
We entered - the pioneers.

Our axes rang in the woodlands,
Where the gaudy bush-birds flew,
And we turned the loam of our newfound home,
Where the Eucalyptus grew.

Housed in the rough log shanty,
Camped in the leaking tent,
From sea to view of the mountains blue
Where the eager diggers went.

We wrought with a will unceasing,
We moulded, and fashioned, and planned
And we fought with the black and we blazed the track
That ye might inherit the land.

There are your shops and churches,
Your cities of stucco and smoke;
And the swift trains fly where the wild cat's cry
O'er the sad bush silence broke.

Take now the fruit of our labour,
Nourish and guard it with care;
For our youth is spent, and our backs are bent
And the snow is in our hair.

Frank Hudson

Answer these questions:

1. Describe some of the skills of these pioneers.

_____

_____

2. What is the poet's hope for those who now live in cities the pioneers have built?

_____

_____

3. Explain how the poet has conveyed the idea of time passing.

_____

_____

4. There is a certain rhythm to this poem that increases the interest and also aids in the feel of the passing of time. Explain what creates this effect.

_____

_____

This poem was written by James Lister Cuthbertson. He was born in Scotland in 1851 and received his education at Oxford. He arrived in Melbourne in 1874. He taught as a Senior Classical Master at Geelong Grammar School, in Victoria from 1875-96.

Read this poem carefully. Think about what James Cuthbertson was saying.

The Australian Sunrise

The Morning Star paled slowly, the Cross hung low to the sea,
And down the shadowy reaches the tide came swirling free,
The lustrous purple blackness of the soft Australian night
Waned in the grey awakening that heralded the light;
Still in the dying darkness, still in the forest dim
The pearly dew of the dawning clung to each giant limb,
Till the sun came up from ocean, red with the cold sea mist,
And smote on the limestone ridges, and the shining tree-tops kissed
Then the fiery Scorpion vanished, the magpie's note was heard,
And the wind in the she-oak wavered and the honeysuckles stirred;
The airy golden vapour rose from the river breast,
The kingfisher came darting out of his crannied nest,
And the bullrushes and reed-beds put off their sallow grey
And burnt with cloudy crimson at the dawning of the day.

The fiery Scorpion refers to the brilliant constellation Scorpio. It contains Antares, a star of the first magnitude, which shines with a reddish light.

Answer these questions:

1. What other constellation of stars is mentioned in this poem?

_____

_____

2. The poet has used colour and contrast in this poem to create a vivid picture. Give several examples of this and explain what effect they have on the reader.

_____

_____

_____

3. The poem rhymes in couplets. How does this aid the poet in his description of sunrise? Re-read the poem and think before you answer.

_____

_____

4. Give two examples of metaphors used in the poem.

_____

_____

5. Reading this poem, do you think the poet enjoyed watching the sun rise on an Australian dawn? Give reasons for your answer.

_____

_____

The final poem is written by Ian Mudie. He *was* born at Hawthorn, South Australia, and worked as an editor and lecturer in creative writing. He made frequent public lectures on Australian literature and regularly conducted the Writers' School at the Adelaide Festival of Arts. He had a realistic view of some of Australia but still loved the land.

Read this poem carefully. It is written from a different perspective.

This Land

Give me a harsh land to wring music from,
brown hills, and dust, with dead grass
straw to my bricks.

Give me words that are cutting-harsh
as wattle-bird notes in dusty gums
crying at noon.

Give me a harsh land, a land that
swings, like heart and blood
from heat to mist.

Give me the hand that like my heart
scorches its flowers of spring,
then floods upon its summer ardour.

Give me a land where rain
is rain that wold beat the heads low,
where wind howls at the windows

and patters dust on tin roofs
while it hides the summer sun
in a mud-red shirt.

Give my words sun and rain
desert and heat and mist
spring flowers and dead grass
blue sea and dusty sky.

song birds and harsh cries
strength and austerity
that this land has.

Answer these questions:

1. This poem is full of contrasting words and phrases. Give at least three examples.

   _____

   _____

2. As you read through this poem, think about the contrasting words the poet has used. What does this tell you about his love for Australia?

   _____

3. The imagery in this poem is very vivid. Give three examples of this imagery and explain its meaning. (Do not repeat the examples you used in question 1.)

   _____

   _____

   _____

   _____

   _____

4. How does the form of the poem help the poet convey his theme?

   _____

   _____

5. Did you enjoy this poem? Explain your answer.

   _____

   _____

Match the Words

Match the words in the box with the definitions.

> villainous, contemporary, prejudice, sufficient, pursue,
> precis, digression, repetition, unanimous, melancholy

1. deviation from the main course   _____

2. continue or proceed along a path   _____

3. summary or extract of text or speech   _____

4. sad or depressed   _____

5. existing or happening at the same period _____

6. the recurrence of an act or event   _____

7. unreasonable opinion or attitude   _____

8. guilty of wicked or criminal behaviour _____

9. enough, adequate   _____

10. all of one opinion   _____

Change to Adjectives

Change the following words to adjectives.

1.	comedy	_____	2.	conclusion	_____
3.	contradiction	_____	4.	ridicule	_____
5.	acquiesce	_____	6.	adversary	_____
7.	absence	_____	8.	humility	_____
9.	deceive	_____	10.	resent	_____

Change to Verbs

Change the following words to verbs.

1.	reconciliation	_____	2.	excellent	_____
3.	hindrance	_____	4.	humility	_____

© Valerie Marett
Coroneos Publications

Australian Homeschooling #563
Successful English 8B

Anachronisms

Writers of historical plays, stories or essays must be on their guard against anachronisms. An anachronism can be defined as "an error in computing time" or "a thing out of harmony with the present." For example, if a novelist described a battle in Viking times and included a Viking armed with an automatic weapon, invented centuries later, he would be guilty of an anachronism. Similarly a story about today should not include Cobb and Co. Coaches, unless the author had staged the scene at a theme park.

Find examples of anachronisms in the following sentences. Rewrite each sentence avoiding the anachronism. There may be more than one.

1. Cleopatra travelled down the Nile in a beautifully decorated river steamer.

   _____

2. The fountain pen, with which John signed the Magna Carta, is now in the British Museum.

   _____

   _____

3. The First World War came to an end in 1918 when the Nazis were forced to seek an armistice.

   _____

   _____

4. Julius Ceasar was stabbed to death on the steps of St. Peter's in Rome.

   _____

5. In 1851 Hargraves used a Geiger-counter to prove that gold was present in the rocks at Summer Hill Creek.

   _____

   _____

6. Napoleon's Old Guard was smashed by tanks at Waterloo.

   _____

7. Australian troops aided Britain in the War of Independence.

   _____

8. Shakespeare based one of his plays on Milton's "Paradise Lost."

   _____

Noun Clauses

A noun clause can not stand alone as an independent sentence although it has a subject and predicate.

Write the noun clause on the line provided and say whether it is the subject, predicate or object of the sentence.

1. The students were in trouble for the mess they made in the hall.

_____

2. I forgot what you said.

_____

3. Whoever first travelled by sea was very brave.

_____

4. The club will give whoever wins the race a gold cup.

_____

5. The solution to the problem was that Margaret would leave early.

_____

6. The audience was amazed by how the trick was done.

_____

7. A cheeseburger is what I ordered.

_____

8. No one knew what to do next.

_____

9. Whatever you choose will be fine.

_____

10. She explained why she couldn't come to the party.

_____

11. What my brother enjoys most is swimming in the sea.

_____

12. Passengers were told why the flight was delayed.

_____

Adverbial Clauses

The chart below shows the different types of adverbial clauses and the <u>subordinating conjunctions</u> that are generally used to connect them to the sentences in which they occur.

Clause	Subordinating Conjunction
Manner	as
Time	when, while, after, before, since, until, whenever, as
Place	where, wherever, whence, whither
Reason	because, and for, as and since (meaning because)
Condition	if, unless, provided, that
Concession	though, although, even if, whether.......... or
Comparison	than
Purpose	so that, in order that, lest
Result	that after "such" and "so"

Each underlined clause is an adverbial clause. State what kind of an adverbial clause it is, and name the word or words it modifies.

1. **When you arrived at the top** of the mountain, there was nothing to do.

   _____

2. It looks very sinister **as only the elements can look when a violent storm is brewing.**

   _____

3. **Because the load was heavy** I groaned from time to time.

   _____

4. **If a fireman relaxes** the hose is likely to whip out of his hand.

   _____

5. Do you think cats are more numerous **than dogs?**

   _____

Shakespeare

Shakespeare was a playwright in the reign of Elizabeth I. He was born on 26th April, 1564 and died 23rd April, 1616. His parents were illiterate but it is believed he entered the *King's New Grammar School* at the age of seven where he worked twelve hours a day, six days a week. He probably left school at age fourteen or fifteen. In 1582 at the age of eighteen he married Anne Hathaway. They had three children.

We are not sure where Shakespeare worked initially but it was probably in a company of travelling actors who toured England. During the 1590's Shakespeare wrote a number of poems as well as some of his well know plays: *Richard III, A Midsummer Night Dream, Romeo and Juliet, The Merchant of Venice* and *Julius Caesar.* He acted in his own plays and those of other poets.

In 1594 he invested in and became part-owner in an acting company, *The Lord Chamberlain's Men.* This meant that as well as acting in the company he had a share in the profits.

The 1600's was his most productive period when he wrote most of his great plays including *Hamlet, Othello, Macbeth* and *King Lear.* From 1603 his company changed its name to *The King's Men* and regularly performed at Court. During this period he bought several properties and became very wealthy. He died just before his fifty-second birthday.

Elizabeth I's reign was a time of prosperity and wealth although life was generally hard for the lower classes. England gained supremacy of the sea: a trade route was opened with Russia, the Spanish Armada was crushed and attempts were made to settle North America. It was during this time Francis Drake sailed around the world.

Elizabeth I was stylish and intelligent and demanded that those around her be intelligent as well. The dress at this time was stiff and uncomfortable. The ladies wore layers and layers of clothing and needed help to dress. Men's clothes were also stiff and uncomfortable. The lower classes' clothes were more flexible and loose fitting with broad brimmed hats and heavy shoes.

The growing prosperity of the time was seen in the growth of theatres, one of the most popular forms of entertainment. Plays before this time were performed in inns, where food and drink was also served. Often behaviour became riotous and the Lord Mayor of London banned theatre performances in the city so they moved to the suburbs. However as time progressed theatres became more respectable.

Theatres were different from today. Many were unroofed. The Globe Theatre was a theatre often associated with Shakespeare's plays. It was octagonal and three stories high. It was an outdoor theatre and could seat up to 3,000 people.

© Valerie Marett
Coroneos Publications

Australian Homeschooling #563
Successful English 8B

Answer these questions:

1. Shakespeare was born _____ and died _____.

2. He was educated at _____.

3. Would this education have made a difference to his life? Explain your answer.

   _____

   _____

   _____

   _____

4. List plays written by Shakespeare that are mentioned in the text.

   _____

   _____

5. What was the name of the theatre often associated with Shakespeare's plays? Describe it.

   _____

   _____

B. Research and write an essay about Elizabethan England. You may choose to give an overall view or just choose something specific about the era. Your essay should be at least 250 words.

C. Choose 2 synonyms for each word below and an antonym where indicated. Make sure the words you choose would fit the context in the text. <u>Do not choose the simplest word you can find.</u>

	Synonym		Antonym
1. prosperity	_____	_____	_____
2. company	_____	_____	
3. property	_____	_____	
4. stiff	_____	_____	_____
5. riotous	_____	_____	_____
6. associated	_____	_____	_____
7. supremacy	_____	_____	

Homonyms

Homonyms are words that are said or spelt the same way as another word but have a different meaning, e.g., wait and weight.

Look at the homonyms below. Write the meaning of each word. Use one of the words in a sentence:

1. aerie: _____

    airy: _____

    _____

2. cereal: _____

    serial: _____

    _____

3. complacent: _____

    complaisant: _____

    _____

4. cue: _____

    queue: _____

5. file: _____

    phial: _____

6. leased: _____

    least: _____

    _____

7. peak: _____

    peek: _____

    pique: _____

8. precedence: _____

    precedents: _____

    presidents: _____

Noun Equivalents

A pronoun is a noun equivalent. Other noun equivalents are:

1. The adjective used as a noun, e.g., The good are always happy.

2. The gerund, e.g., <u>Surfing</u> has become a popular pastime.
We like <u>surfing</u> during the summer months.

3. The noun-infinitive, e.g., <u>To keep</u> silent is often too difficult.
I desire <u>to dream</u> away an hour or two.

4. The noun phrase, e.g., <u>What to wear</u> is my problem.
Do you know <u>how to study</u> effectively?

5. The noun clause, e.g., <u>Why Brian acted in that way</u> puzzled his friends.
They all thought <u>that Brian behaved foolishly.</u>

Noun equivalents can be used as either the subject or the object.

Complete the sentence using the type of noun equivalent asked for in the bracket.

1. He preferred .... on the generosity of others. (gerund)

   _____

2. I like .... novels and adventure stories. (noun-infinitive)

   _____

3. Our captain knows .... (noun clause)

   _____

4. Only the ....deserve the fair. (adjective)

   _____

5. Who dislikes ....? (gerund or noun-infinitive)

   _____

6. Realising .... we took to the boats. (noun clause)

   _____

7. ....on the kindness of others for a job was his plan. (gerund)

   _____

8. The .... should help the .... (adjective)

   _____

© Valerie Marett
Coroneos Publications

Australian Homeschooling #563
Successful English 8B

Background to Australian Settlement

Prior to settlement in Australia huge changes took place in Britain. Until the middle of the eighteenth century the method of farming was much the same as that used in the Middle Ages. It was an open field system where one in four fields always lay fallow. This was wasteful and there was much loss of time going from one strip to another. (If you remember villagers had strips of land divided over several unfenced fields.) This method was also unprogressive as farming was done on a communal basis and every man had to farm in the same way.

In the eighteenth and nineteenth century there was a tremendous rise in population, due in part to advances in medicine, and an improved standard of living. This increase was phenomenal and without an increase in agriculture and industry it would not have been possible to maintain the populace.

Between 1700 and 1850 land was fenced and redistributed under the Enclosure Acts creating compact farms. This led to experimentation to increase the productivity of the land. Farms became larger as wealthy land owners bought up farms and the existing farmers became tenant farmers. Those left with no land became farm labourers or moved to the towns.

This was a period during which there were many inventions. The Seed Drill invented in 1701 allowed corn to be sown in regular rows and with less scattering of seed reducing that eaten by birds. The Rotherham plough in 1703 turned the soil more efficiently and in 1827 the first reaping machine was invented which made cutting corn less labour intensive than cutting using a scythe.

Rotating crops further increased annual production. In the early 1700's Viscount Townsend used a four crop rotation system to improve soil fertility. Clover, lucerne and other leguminous plants were also used. This development meant that it was no longer necessary to leave a field fallow every two to three years to allow nutrients to replenish the soil.

From the 1750's farmers built underground dung pits to hold and preserved animal manure. This manure, when added to the top soil, helped produce an increase in crop yield. Deep trenches were dug for drainage, which meant that the crops were less waterlogged, resulting in higher productivity and profits. Selective breeding was practised from the 1750's, leading to better yields of milk and higher quality and quantity of meat and wool.

The increase in the number of urban dwellers who were dependant on farmers for food made these changes necessary. This led to the purchase of land by the middle class who wanted to make profits from farming and therefore employed modern methods. Improvements in transport made it easier for farmers to transport food to the towns and receive deliveries of coal and machinery.

As a result of the Napoleonic Wars leading to reduced supplies of corn from Europe, the local price of corn increased. Higher prices provided an incentive to produce more.

A. Word Knowledge. Find a word that means the following:

1. land left unseeded for one year or more _____

2. highly extraordinary, exceptional _____

3. relating to plants of the pea family containing root nodules able to fix nitrogen _____

4. a tool with a long curved blade used for cutting crops _____

5. a substance that provides nourishment suitable for the maintenance of life and growth _____

B. Answer these questions:

1. Describe the type of farming used in the Middle Ages.

_____

_____

2. Think! What were the results of the Enclosure Act?

_____

_____

_____

_____

3. Explain how either the Seed Drill, the Rotherham Plough or rotating crops increased production.

_____

_____

_____

4. Improvements other than those discussed in question 3 were made. Explain two of them.

_____

_____

_____

5. Did all these changes in agriculture help Britain to survive the European Blockade by Napoleon? Explain your answer.

_____

_____

© Valerie Marett
Coroneos Publications

Australian Homeschooling #563
Successful English 8B

Understanding Shakespeare

Shakespeare wrote thirty-seven plays and one hundred and fifty four sonnets. His plays can be divided into comedies, tragedies, histories and romances. Below you will find the most commonly known plays in each category.

Comedies
The Merchant of Venice
Much Ado About Nothing
Midsummer Night's Dream
The Taming of the Shrew
Twelfth Night

Tragedies
Anthony and Cleopatra
Hamlet
Julius Caesar
King Lear
Macbeth
Othello
Romeo and Juliet

Histories
Richard II
Richard III
Henry IV part 1 and 2
Henry V
Henry VI part 1, 2 and 3

Romances
The Winter's Tale
The Tempest
Cymbeline
Pericles

Shakespeare wrote in the language of his day so some of the words and the way a sentence is written may seem strange but it shouldn't deter you from reading at least one play by Shakespeare. "No Fear" versions of most of his plays are available on the internet. They show the play as it is written on one page and a modern translation on the next. While these can be referred to, it is best to have a printed copy.

To choose a play, read a synopsis of each play and decide which play you would prefer to study. Check if a DVD is available for this book as this may also help you understand and enjoy the play.

Shakespeare was a true genius with words. His plays are clever, witty, deep, dramatic, sometimes funny and he has been read by scholars and students for centuries because his plays tell so much about life, love and human nature (and

© Valerie Marett
Coroneos Publications

Australian Homeschooling #563
Successful English 8B

human nature does not change.)

When studying Shakespeare watch a DVD or a play of the Shakespearean play you have chosen before you start. Then read the play once right through. Go back and look at it again, breaking each section down. Remember it is a play so it may help to read it aloud.

Look at each of the plays below. Say what category it falls in: comedy, tragedy, history or romance.

1. King Lear   _____

2. The Tempest   _____

3. Romeo and Juliet   _____

4. Richard III   _____

5. Midsummer Night's Dream   _____

Some tips in reading and understanding Shakespeare

1. **Do not pause at the end of the line unless there is a punctuation mark.**
   Shakespeare's verse has a rhythm of its own and is natural to speak.

   Romeo and Juliet: Romeo is speaking of Juliet in Scene 5 starting at line 9.

   O,(pause) she doth teach the torches to burn bright! (pause)
   It seems she hangs upon the cheeks of night
   Like a rich jewel in an Ehtiop's ear; (pause)

2. **The punctuation marks help to define the thought.** Try and understand each speech as you read it.

   The prologue in *Romeo and Juliet* sets the scene before the play starts.

   Two households, both alike in dignity,
   In fair Verona, where we lay our scene,
   From ancient grudge break to new mutiny,
   Where civil blood makes civil hands unclean.
   From forth the fatal loins of these two foes
   A pair of star crossed lovers take their life;

   "Two households..... scene" is the first thought which tells us the play is set in the city of Verona and is about two families.

   The second thought is "From...... unclean." We learn that there are two families with a long standing hatred that erupts into further violence .

   The final thought is "From forth....their life." We learn that an unlucky child from each family falls in love and ends up committing suicide.

3. As you read longer sentences **keep track of who did what to whom,** (subject, verb and object.)

   For example, in a "*Midsummer Night's Dream,*" Scene 1, lines 1-6.

   THESEUS
   Now, fair Hippolyta, our nuptial hour
   Draws on apace. Four happy days bring in
   Another moon. But oh, methinks how slow
   This old moon wanes! She lingers my desires,
   Like to a stepdame or a dowager
   Long withering out a young man's revenue

   In lines 1 and 2 Theseus speaks to Hippolyta and tells her that soon they will be married. (Hippolyta—subject, nuptial hour, i.e. wedding—object.)

   Lines 2-3 "*Four happy days....moon*" Theseus continues to talk about the wedding which will be in four days when there is a new moon.

   Lines 3-6 "But oh,..... revenue" Theseus continues to speak about the moon and how, because he is wanting the next four days to pass quickly, the moon seems so slow in fading away.

4. **Sometimes a word or a phrase is left out. This is called an ellipsis.**
   For example, Benvolio asks Romeo's father and mother if they know what is bothering their son, Romeo.

   Romeo's father answers:
   "*I neither know it nor can learn of him*"

   What he is saying is "I neither know [the cause of] it, nor can [I] learn [about it from] him."

5. **Language has changed over the years.** Below are a brief list of words Shakespeare commonly used and their meaning.

   anon = right now
   aye/yea + yes
   e'en = evening
   fare-thee-well = goodbye
   hath = has
   morrow = tomorrow
   n'er = never
   pray/ prithee = please
   thee = you
   thou = you
   verily = truthfully
   wherefore = why

   art = are
   dost or doth = does or do
   ere = before
   hark = listen
   hither = here
   nay = no
   oft = often
   perchance = perhaps
   thine/thy = your
   thyself = yourself
   whence = from where

From the list of plays on page 108 choose two plays. Discover what each play is about. Write a summary of the plot of each play. Hint: many of the "No Fear Shakespeare" posts on the internet provide you with a summary of the play. **Do not** copy them. Write the summary in your own words.

1. _____
_____
_____
_____
_____
_____
_____
_____
_____
_____
_____
_____
_____

2. _____
_____
_____
_____
_____
_____
_____
_____
_____
_____
_____
_____
_____
_____
_____
_____
_____

Australian Homeschooling #563
Successful English 8B

Hyphens, Brackets and Dashes

Hyphens

A hypen links words or word parts that act as one. Some uses are:

1. **Hyphenate a word when** they come before a noun they modify and act as a single idea. This is called a compound adjective.

   For example: an off-campus apartment
   state-of-the-art design

2. **A hyphen may join two nouns to make a compound noun.**

   For example: sister-in-law

3. **It must be used when a word is broken at the end of a line. It must divide at the end of a syllable.**

   For example: The Industrial Revolution also produced <u>manufactur-</u>
   <u>ers,</u> who were often more wealthy than the aristocracy,

Rewrite the sentence adding a hyphen when necessary.

1. My great grandfather fought in World War 1.

   _____

2. Please return the completed form in a self addressed envelope.

   _____

3. Now I am at university I am semi independent.

   _____

Brackets

1. **Brackets, also called parenthesis, are always used in pairs to set off matter that is not part of the main statement.**

   For example: Eat a green vegetable (spinach, beans or peas) every day.

2. **Brackets are used to set off numbers or letters in an outline or list.**

   For example: (1) Research and Development
   (2) Production

3. **Punctuation marks are normally placed after the bracketed material.**

> For example: If you like cooking (I hate it), here is a good recipe.

But **if the whole sentence is in brackets, final full stops, question marks etc. are placed within the brackets.**

> For example: (By the way, I thought the idea was good.)

Rewrite the sentence adding brackets when necessary.

1. Do you like rich food even if it's bad for you?

   _____

2. The other man David Johnson refused to make a statement.

   _____

3. He had three interests in life: a his work b his children c golf.

   _____

Dash

1. **A dash is used to represent the omission of a word or part of a word.**

> For example: Mr S——— , who is suspected of stealing, has left town.

2. **A dash is used between numbers or words to mean until or through.**

> For example: William Blake (1757—1827) was a great English poet.

3. **A dash is used to distinguish a word, or a group of words, from the rest of the sentence when it is introduced unexpectedly and is not structurally part of the sentence.**

> For example: Colin had a clever idea—but, here, read the report for yourself.

4. **A dash is used before a specific list or example that explains some word or phrase used in the first part of the sentence.**

> For example: Have you met the Smiths—Mary and Paul?

Rewrite the sentence adding a dash when necessary.

1. For tonight's homework read chapters 16 24.

   _____

2. Be sure to bring some warm clothes among other things a jumper and woollen socks.

   _____

Background to Australian Settlement 2

As the agricultural revolution progressed many of the poor lost their homes and were forced to move to the towns where a revolution in industry, even more remarkable than that in agriculture, was taking place.

Originally wool had been sent to Flanders, modern day Belgium, but gradually the English began to produce their own cloth. At first this was heavy and coarse, but a number of skilled workers from Europe, who arrived due to religious persecution, took refuge in England and passed on their skills so by the seventeenth century, England was making all kinds of woollen cloth.

During this period iron was smelted with wood charcoal, which made iron very expensive and it was only used sparingly. Coal was mined in various parts of the country, but it was too expensive to be widely used. There was also no good method of pumping water out of the coal pits. The invention of James Watt's steam pump in 1765 solved this problem.

Most of the manufactured goods were originally produced in home industries at the close of the seventeenth century. In the country, small farmers added to their earnings by spinning and weaving in their homes and selling them in the towns. In the towns the Masters had apprentices that worked in the master's home. This domestic system had certain advantages: there was a great demand for the goods and cottage workers became prosperous; the work was well done but was produced in a more leisurely way; those who manufactured goods were sure of selling them. On the other hand there were certain disadvantages: there was no uniformity in the quality of the goods; workers only worked when it suited them, so merchants found it hard to get the goods they required.

Gradually great changes started to take place, largely due to the demand of the colonies for more goods. Production needed to increased. The greatest changes took place between the middle of the eighteenth and nineteenth century. It took place in Britain for many reasons. Coal and iron were available and easily transported. The coalfields of Britain were larger than any in Germany and France and closer to important harbours. In addition there was plenty of water in the north and north-west that could be used for water power and the moist climate of the Midlands was well suited to dealing with raw cotton.

England's geographical position was sound: she was the centre of the industrial world. She had a number of colonies who were demanding manufactured goods in ever increasing quantities and which provided her with immense quantities of raw material. She had ships and was able to carry a huge amount of trade and had not been ravaged by war, as Europe had.

In addition the governing aristocracy, unlike that of Europe, were interested in commerce, and did not despise fortunes made in factories or mines. As a result they entered into every form of industrial and commercial enterprise. The Industrial Revolution also produced manufacturers, who were often more wealthy than the aristocracy, and who employed a huge number of workers.

A. Answer these questions:

1. From where did workers skilled in producing cloth arrive and why did they leave their own country?

   _____

   _____

2. Think! Why would cheap iron and coal have made an industrial revolution possible?

   _____

   _____

   _____

3. Give two reasons why goods were produced at a slower rate in small cottage industries goods.

   _____

   _____

4. What were the main reasons that there was increased production?

   _____

   _____

5. List other reasons for increased production.

   _____

   _____

   _____

   _____

   _____

B. Word Knowledge. Find a word that means the following:

1. vast, substantial   _____

2. hereditary ruling class, nobility   _____

3. oppression because of religious belief   _____

C. Research and write.

Research and write about the lives of workers in the coal mines during the Industrial Revolution.

Find the Word

Rewrite the sentence, replacing the underlined word with a word from the box that has similar meaning.

cited, eminent, intercede, acquiesced, prolific, turbulent, authentic, allusion, hilarious, adversary, ludicrous, notorious

1. The boxer's **opponent** was formidable.

   _____

2. The waves were **full of violent movement.**

   _____

3. He possessed a **genuine** Roman coin.

   _____

4. The highwayman was **infamous.**

   _____

5. A **distinguished** heart surgeon performed the operation.

   _____

6. The chancellor of the university **consented without protest** to the lecturers' demands.

   _____

7. T.S. Elliot made an **indirect reference** to Hamlet.

   _____

8. The nurse tried to **plead or act on behalf of another.**

   _____

9. The actor's performance was **very funny.**

   _____

10. The solicitor **quoted as reference** an old Act.

    _____

11. The newspaper article was **absurd.**

    _____

12. Dr Zeus was a **very productive** writer of children's books.

    _____

Synonyms

Match each word on the left with a synonym on the right.

1. initiate	a. confirm
2. scheme	b. proficient
3. sombre	c. destructive
4. adept	d. commence
5. schedule	e. displeasure
6. lethal	f. conspire
7. chagrin	g. solemn
8. deluge	h. supplicate
9. pursue	i. timetable
10. implore	j. accept
11. hoard	k. inundate
12. lithe	l. stockpile
13. accede	m. supple
14. ratify	n. chase

Antonyms

Match each word on the left with a synonym on the right.

1. secluded	a. permanent
2. miser	b. changeable
3. transient	c. establishment
4. abundance	d. accessible
5. immutable	e. scarcity
6. abolition	g. philanthropist

Shakespearean Tragedy

Shakespeare's tragedies were influenced by Greek tragedy and Aristotle's notion of drama, which depicted the downfall of a hero or famous character. Most of the tragedies written by Shakespeare are ambition and revenge tragedies, e.g., Othello, Hamlet, King Lear and Macbeth. The exception is Romeo and Juliet, which is a romantic tragedy where the two main characters, Romeo and Juliet, both from feuding families, fall in love. Romeo acts impulsively without thinking of consequences, which causes separation of the lovers and ultimately their death.

Shakespeare's tragedies share a number of common features.

a. **a tragic flaw:** A tragic flaw is a personality trait that leads to the downfall of the protagonist, i.e., the main character in the story. The catastrophe must not be the result of an accident, but must be brought about by some essential trait in the character of the hero or heroine acting either directly or through its effect on other persons. This is the most important element and almost every hero or heroine of a Shakespearean tragedy possesses this tragic flaw. Examples of this are Othello's jealousy, Hamlet's indecisiveness and Macbeth's obsession with power.

The hero must nonetheless have in him something which outweighs his defects and keep the audience interested in him enough to care about his fate.

b. **Supernatural Elements:** The use of supernatural elements is a common characteristic of Elizabethan plays. In Shakespeare's plays supernatural powers contribute to the fate of the protagonist, but are not solely responsible for his downfall. This still lies in the actions of the hero. These supernatural elements are not illusions in the mind of the hero as they contribute to the action of the play with their presence in more than one or two scenes. The use of witches in Macbeth reflect the belief in evil powers who practise evil rites to affect the central character. When Macbeth encounters the three witches he starts believing whatever they say without questioning their existence.

c. **Internal and External Conflict:** The external conflict is the conflict between two people, the hero and another main character of the story. It can also be the conflict between two parties, one of which is led by the hero. The result of the conflict is always in favour of the other party as it is the good party.

The inward struggle of the hero is in his mind. The result of this struggle is often that the hero goes insane, for example, in King Lear the king becomes mentally ill.

d. **Fate or Fortune:** since the tragic hero or heroine is of high estate and is a public figure, his or her downfall affects not only his or her personal life, but the fate and welfare of the entire nation. It reflects the powerlessness of human beings and the omnipotence of fate that the story of someone of low estate could not produce. The adverse effects of fate on an empire are evident in Macbeth when Malcom and McDuff are planning to defeart Macbeth, and at the same time trying to support a collapsing kingdom. McDuff suggests Malcolm takes the throne, but Malcom is not mature enough to hold the falling empire.

e. **The theme of foul and revenge:** "Fair is foul, and foul is fair" pervades throughout Macbeth, reminding the audience they need to look deeper in order to understand the thoughts and actions of the characters. Though it first appears in the beginning in the twelfth line of *Act I, Scene I*, uttered by witches as "*Fair is foul, foul is fair*"; however, it lasts throughout the story with recurring themes of evil acts and deception in the name of equivocation, ambition and good. The meaning of this line is that though events, things and people may seem good or bad, after careful examination, they turn out to be opposite.

Similarly, in Hamlet, revenge is the theme built from the start of the play and making it the driving force behind the character of Hamlet.

f. **Paradox of life:** Shakespeare's tragedies reflect the paradox of life in that the calamity and suffering experienced by the hero are contrasted with his previous happiness and glory. In Macbeth, for example, Macbeth is portrayed as the most brave and loyal soldier of the nation. However Macbeth is not satisfied with what he has and wants more. This desire leads him to think evilly and act on it, which is the opposite of his real character.

Answer the following questions.

1. List the common features in Shakespeare's tragedies.

_____

_____

_____

_____

_____

_____

2. Look back at your summaries on page 111. If you have summarised a tragedy, list the features mentioned in these pages that apply.

_____

_____

_____

_____

Commas vs Semi-Colons

Use a semi-colon when a full stop is possible but would separate the sentences too strongly.

- **a semicolon is used to separate two or more grammatically complete sentences that are closely connected in thought.**
  For example: I said it would rain today; it seems I wasn't far wrong.

- **a semicolon may be used before such words as *nevertheless, however, hence, instead, yet, thus, for example* and *consequently.***
  For example: We had a late start; nevertheless we got to the airport on time.

- **A semicolon may be used to separate the items of a list; or to separate groups of words from other related groups of words if there are commas within the group; or to separate the various self-contained parts of a very long sentence.**
  For example: You will find references to herb gardens on pages 4, 38, 43 and 72; to wild herbs on page 18, 37 and 42.

  The winning numbers were 14,273; 36,663; and 25,370.

Each of the following sentences needs either a comma or semicolon or both. Put in the necessary punctuation.

1. The hill was covered with wildflowers it was a beautiful sight.

2. The house was clean the table set and the porch light on everything was ready for the guests' arrival.

3. As I turned around I heard a loud thump for the cat had upset the goldfish bowl.

4. I thought registration day would be tiring but I didn't know I would have to stand in so many lines.

5. Many companies make sugar-free soft drinks that are flavoured by artificial chemicals the drinks usually contain only one or two calories per serving.

6. Mr Green the plumber George Crompton the painter and Bill Stephens were at the party.

7. The little boy was bright for example he could already do division.

8. The bus stop worse luck was three blocks away and Jim thoroughly drenched by the rain headed for it at a gallop.

9. The dog growling and snarling snapped at me I was so frightened that I ran.

Confusing Pairs

Complete these sentences by inserting the correct word (from the brackets) into the blank spaces.

1. The _____ witness failed to appear in court. (principle, principal)

2. If one is proved guilty of negligent driving, one is _____ to face a severe fine. (libel, liable)

3. For a mere pittance the inventor sold his _____ labour saving device. (ingenious, ingenuous)

4. His colleagues found his _____ attitude very annoying since he was not very good at his job. (complacent, complaisant)

5. The Government's anti-inflation policy was a _____ factor in high unemployment.   (causal, casual)

6. The barrister _____ six precedents in his argument. (sighted, cited, sited)

7. Germany _____ territory to Poland in 1945.   (seeded, ceded)

8. The audience was enthralled as the play reached the _____ scene.   (climactic, climatic)

9. Relations between the two countries broke down and war seemed

   _____ .   (immanent, imminent)

10. The noise near the road works is quite _____. (intolerant, intolerable)

11. The Government's _____ policy has been severely restricted. (monetary, monitory)

12. _____ with care over the rough road. (precede, proceed)

13. The scientists _____ on the research project. (collaborated, corroborated)

14. He was a pacifist who spoke _____ against the war from 1939 to 1945. (consistently, constantly)

15. Being absorbed in his scientific studies, he was _____ in football. (disinterested, uninterested)

16. The old building was _____ by a bomb. (raised, razed, rise)

Background to Australian Settlement 3

Industrial changes led to a tremendous increase in trade and this increase in trade brought great wealth to the upper and middle classes of English society in the eighteenth and nineteenth centuries. The wealthy increased their wealth and became masters of industry, striving to buy raw material cheaply, paying small wages and then selling and making a good profit. Hired labourers were less important than the machinery as there were plenty more workers to replace them.

The working class suffered badly under this system. Skilled workers were no longer needed and there was a great demand for women and children to do the necessary work. Children especially were nimbler, cheaper and easy to manage. Very often pauper children were sold in batches to factory or mill owners and the conditions under which they lived and worked were appalling. They often worked a 14-18 hour day and were paid small wages.

Conditions in the cities, which often sprang up around these factories, were atrocious. Houses were hovels, far too small for one family and yet often containing several. They were filthy and little effort was made at personal cleanliness. The smoke-ridden air of the cities made health worse and disease was rife. Primitive sanitation, lack of pure water, rubbish left in the street to rot and little fresh air brought fever and disease.

Yet despite these conditions, the population continued to increase and the movement from the country to the town where the factories lay continued. The employers frequently abused their power and there were no restrictions concerning wages, hours of labour, or age of employees. Parliament was not representative and was controlled by nobles and millionaire merchants. However this situation gradually changed. Conditions were improved by the passing of the Factories Act and Mines Act and by the growth of democracy and trade unions, who fought for shorter hours and higher wages.

New methods of transport were developed without which the Industrial Revolution could not have continued. Although there were many canals on the Continent there was only one in England. After 1760, transport canals were built on a large scale throughout England to carry materials.

Roads throughout England were notoriously bad. Parishes were supposed to pay for their upkeep but rarely did. During the 18th Century the method of financing them was changed to a Turnpike Trust. Turnpikes and toll houses were set up to collect money from those using the roads. Technical changes were brought about by John Metcalfe, Thomas Telford and John McAdam. Metcalfe produced stone laid roads and bridges and McAdam and Telford both produced smooth, hard surfaces that made roads easier to use.

Railways started appearing and this caused a catastrophic decline in coaches. By 1846 there were 11,265 kilometres of railway track in England carrying people, raw products and goods. In addition trains broke down local barriers and familiarised people with machinery.

A. Word Knowledge. Find a word that means the following:

1. ruinous, calamitous   _____

2. appalling, dreadful   _____

3. widespread, common   _____

4. agile, dexterous   _____

5. indigent, destitute   _____

B. Answer these questions:

1. In your own words explain why the working class suffered badly as a result of the Industrial Revolution.

    _____

    _____

    _____

    _____

2. Think. What are the two most important factors affecting health in cities today? Were these needs served in the poorer section of the cities during the Industrial Revolution?

    _____

    _____

3. List the changes that improved the conditions of the workers.

    _____

    _____

4. The continued development of the Industrial Revolution was possible because of the development of new methods of transport. Explain what these methods were.

    _____

    _____

    _____

5. Think. Why did railways cause a catastrophic decline in coaches?

    _____

    _____

Find the Word

Fill in the space with a word from the box.

> beverage, extrovert, cadaverous, etiquette, gourmet,
> didactic, surrender, elite, exorbitant, palatable

1. give up _____

2. like a dead person _____

3. inclined to lecture others too much _____

4. able to be eaten _____

5. hot chocolate as a drink _____

6. the accepted code of good manners _____

7. a special privileged group _____

8. one whose personality is outgoing _____

9. an expert in matters of taste in food _____

10. excessive, especially in cost _____

Clichés

A cliché is a phrase or opinion that is overused and betrays a lack of original thought. Match up the clichés in the left hand column with their correct meaning in the right hand column.

1. to keep one's nose to the grindstone	a. to be in charge
2. to put one's foot down	b. to make a peace overture
3. to rest on one's laurels	c. someone treacherous
4. to rule the roost	d. to work extremely hard
5. to show a clean pair of heels	e. to be content with past successes
6. to skate on thin ice	f. having the same faults
7. a snake in the grass	g. to act dangerously
8. a storm in a teacup	h. to run away
9. tarred with the same brush	i. a great fuss over nothing
10. to hold out an olive branch	j. to make a firm stand

Australian Homeschooling #563
Successful English 8B

Add a Subject and a Main Clause

Correct these incomplete sentences by adding a <u>subject</u> for the participle to be attached to and a <u>main clause.</u> You may add it before or after the participial phrase. The first is completed for you.

1. Planning each manoeuvre with meticulous care.
   <u>John, planning each manoeuvre with meticulous care, choreographed the ballet.</u>

2. Buzzing with excitement at the sudden change in the game.

   _____

   _____

3. Burning with desire to solve the riddle of the river's source.

   _____

   _____

4. Watched by viewers all across the world.

   _____

   _____

Compound Sentences

Turn the sentences and incomplete sentences below into compound sentences.

1. The trees are beautiful native species. They are mainly varieties of the eucalyptus family.

   _____

   _____

2. My mind was fuzzy and all sorts of funny things seemed to be happening to me. For example, I seemed to be floating, and I felt as light as a feather.

   _____

   _____

3. I remember very vividly my first attempt at skiing. Especially the sprained ankle and the hospital they took me to.

   _____

   _____

Shakespeare's Histories and Comedies

Common features of Shakespeare's histories

a. **focus on English monarchs:** Shakespeare's history plays basically revolved around the lives of English kings. The exceptions are Julius Caesar and Antony and Cleopatra, which were written about Roman history.

The plays were written during the reign of Elizabeth I, a Tudor, and therefore generally play upon Elizabethan propaganda showing the danger of civil war and glorifying the Queen's Tudor ancestors. These history plays chronical medieval power struggles encompassing five generations. They dramatise the Hundred Years War with France from Henry V to Joan of Arc. They also depict the War of Roses fought between York and Lancaster.

b. **not historically accurate:** While these plays are not always historically accurate, Shakespeare was not aiming for historical accuracy, but was writing for the entertainment of a theatre audience and therefore moulded historical events to suit his purpose.

c. **explores the social structure of the time:** Shakespeare's plays offer a view of society that cuts right across the class system. These plays present all kind of characters from lowly beggars to the monarchy. It is not uncommon for characters from both ends of the social strata to play scenes together, e.g., Henry V and Falstaff who appear in a number of plays.

d. **represent the compromise of life:** The play may end in catastrophe or triumph, but the catastrophe is apt to be undignified and the triumph won at a price. They provide an equal measure of comedy and tragedy.

Common features of Shakespeare's comedies

The difference between a comedy and a tragedy is that comedies treat subjects lightly. They often use puns, metaphors and insults to provoke laughter. The comedy usually has a happy ending. The main characteristics are:

a. **a struggle of young lovers to overcome problems:** Love provides the main ingredient for the plot. If the lovers are unmarried when the play opens, either they have not met or there is some obstacle in the way of their love, for example, the slanderous tongues that nearly wreck love in "Much Ado About Nothing;"the father insistent on the daughter marrying his choice in "A Mid-Summer Night's Dream."

b. The **plot** is very important in Shakespeare's comedies. They are often very convoluted, twisted and confusing and extremely hard to follow.

c. **themes of love and friendship:** these are played within a courtly society.

© Valerie Marett
Coroneos Publications

Australian Homeschooling #563
Successful English 8B

d.   **discord and resolution:** at the beginning of the play there is always an element of discord, which is resolved before the close. The hero of the play represents society as a whole and because of this we get at the end a sense of the hero living happily ever after.

e.   **Hero:** the hero rarely appears in the opening lines although we hear about him from other characters. The hero is virtuous and strong, but always possesses a character flaw.

f.   number of **acts**: all of Shakespeare's comedies have 5 acts. The climax of the play is always during the third act.

g.   **characters:** Shakespearean plays always contain a wide variety of characters. Some are only seen briefly and never seen again. His female leads are usually described as petite and often assume male disguises. Often foul weather will parallel the motional state of the characters. The audience is often informed of events before the characters, and any future meeting does not happen immediately.

h.   **language:** Shakespeare comedies are peppered with clever word play, metaphors and insults.

i.   **ethical principles:** like a tragedy, there is a collision with some ethical principle on the part of the individual; he intends to violate these principles but does not realise his intention; he is foiled through external deception, or breaks down through internal weakness; the character in comedy, unlike the one in tragedy does not have the great absorption in some great purpose.

Answer the following questions.

1. List the common features in Shakespeare's comedies.

_____

_____

_____

_____

_____

_____

_____

_____

_____

_____

© Valerie Marett
Coroneos Publications

Australian Homeschooling #563
Successful English 8B

2. List the common features in Shakespeare's histories.

_____

_____

_____

_____

3. Look back at your summaries on page 111. If you have summarised a comedy or an historical play, list the features mentioned in these pages that apply.

_____

_____

_____

_____

_____

_____

_____

Word Association

Think of a word that would be associated with the following phrases. The first letter or two have been given to you.

1. dead   <u>c</u><u>orpse</u>

2. rapid spread of disease   ep_____

3. to reject   re_____

4. brain injury   con_____

5. restrain or check   in_____

6. one who sells spectacles   op_____

7. disease of the lungs   pn_____

8. highly likely to be caught (disease)   in_____

9. not having any serious purpose   fr_____

Shakespearean Devices

Shakespeare used various techniques throughout his plays both to inform his readers and heighten the effects of the play. Some of these are:

Prologue

Elizabethan dramatists were influenced by the tradition of prologues in Greek and Roman plays and included it in their plays. A prologue in Elizabethan plays helped to quieten and settle down the audience and prepared them for the events they were to witness in the performance. Usually the actor who read the prologue was dressed in more sombre clothes to differentiate him from the other actors who were in colourful costumes.

The extract of a prologue below is taken from "Henry V."

> *Oh, for a muse of fire that would ascend*
> *The brightest heaven of invention!*
> *A kingdom for a stage, princes to act,*
> *And monarchs to behold the swelling scene!*
> *Then should the warlike Harry, like himself,*
> *Assume the port of Mars, and at his heels,*
> *Leashed in like hounds, should famine, sword, and fire*
> *Crouch for employment. But pardon, gentles all,*
> *The flat unraised spirits that hath dared*
> *On this unworthy scaffold to bring forth*
> *So great an object. Can this cockpit hold*
> *The vasty fields of France? Or may we cram*
> *Within this wooden O the very casques*
> *That did affright the air at Agincourt?*
> *O pardon, since a crooked figure may*
> *Attest in little place a million,*
> *And let us, ciphers to this great account,*
> *On your imaginary forces work.*

The playwright is asking the audience to forgive the fact that he can not present the battle as it really was because of the size of the stage. If he could then he would present King Henry as he really was. Since Shakespeare can not do this he begs the audience to use their imagination to overcome any short comings.

Soliloquy

The word "soliloquy" means "talking to oneself. It is a devise that Shakespeare used to allow a character to communicate his or her thoughts directly to the audience. The character may be surrounded by other characters, but Elizabethan audiences took for granted the fact that no-one else could hear him or her.

One of the most famous of Shakespeare's soliloquys is spoken by Hamlet in Act 3, Scene 1, where Hamlet weighs the pros or cons of ending his life.

© Valerie Marett
Coroneos Publications

Australian Homeschooling #563
Successful English 8B

To be, or not to be? That is the question—
Whether 'tis nobler in the mind to suffer
The slings and arrows of outrageous fortune,
Or to take arms against a sea of troubles,
And, by opposing, end them? To die, to sleep—
No more—and by a sleep to say we end
The heartache and the thousand natural shocks
That flesh is heir to—'tis a consummation
Devoutly to be wished! To die, to sleep.
To sleep, perchance to dream—ay, there's the rub,
For in that sleep of death what dreams may come
When we have shuffled off this mortal coil,
Must give us pause. There's the respect
That makes calamity of so long life.

Monologue

A monologue is a speech made by a character to other characters or sometimes to a crowd. Shakespeare's plays are full of monologues. The most famous is in Henry V in Act 3, Scene 1, where the king is leading his troops into battle.

Once more unto the breach, dear friends, once more;
Or close the wall up with our English dead!
In peace there's nothing so becomes a man,
As modest stillness and humility;
But when the blast of war blows in our ears,
Then imitate the action of the tiger:
Stiffen the sinews, conjure up the blood,
Disguise fair nature with hard-favoured rage:
Then lend the eye a terrible aspect;
Let it pry through the portage of the head,
Like the brass cannon; let the brow o'erwhelm it
As fearfully as doth a galled rock
O'erhang and jutty his confounded base,
Swill'd with the wild and wasteful ocean.
Now set the teeth and stretch the nostril wide;
Hold hard the breath and bend up every spirit
To his full height. On, on, you noblest English,
Whose blood is fet from fathers of war-proof!
Fathers that, like so many Alexanders,
Have in these parts from morn till even fought,
And sheathed their swords for lack of argument.
Dishonour not your mothers: now attest,
That those whom you call'd fathers did beget you.
Be copy now to men of grosser blood,
And teach them how to war. And you, good yeoman,
Whose limbs were made in England, show us here
The mettle of your pasture: let us swear
That you are worth your breeding; which I doubt not;
For there is none of you so mean and base,
That hath not noble lustre in your eyes.

I see you stand like greyhounds in the slips,
Straining upon the start. The game's afoot:
Follow your spirit; and upon this charge,
Cry 'God for Harry! England! and Saint George!'

Metaphors and Similes

Shakespeare uses metaphors a great deal and similes occasionally. When Romeo says of Juliet,

"O, she doth teach the torches to burn bright!
Her beauty hangs upon the cheek of night,
Like a rich jewel in an Ethiop's ear,"

These three lines contain two metaphors, and one simile. Juliet cannot be said literally to teach the torches anything; but her brightness may be said to make them, or rather the owner of them, ashamed of their dimness; or she may be said to be so radiant, that the torches, or the owner of them, may learn from her how torches ought to shine. Neither can it be said literally that her beauty hangs upon the cheek of night, for the night has no cheek; but it may be said to bear the same relation to the night as a diamond pendant does to the dark cheek that sets it off. Then the last line is a simile; what is therein expressed being likened to a rich jewel hanging in an Ethiop's ear.

Something to Do:

Choose a play written by Shakespeare. Review all the things you have learnt about Shakespeare. Study the play you have chosen and then write an analysis of the play. You should include most of the following:

- whether it is a tragedy, comedy, romance or history
- protagonist's identity
- other important characters
- the plot
- elements included in the play, e.g., tragic flaw
- devices used by Shakespeare: soliloquy, monologue, metaphors

Answers Successful English 8B

Page 3
Using the Best Word: Correct Synonym
1. frail
2. clamour
3. earthy
4. omen
5. lethargic
6. clamour
7. cleaved
8. intemperate
9. occult
10. occasional

Page 4
Principal and Subordinate Clause

1. **Principal clause:** Margaret hummed a song to herself
   Subordinate clause: When painting

2. **Principal clause:** John takes his time
   Subordinate clause: when reading a menu

3. **Principal clause:** we should start a recycling programme
   Subordinate clause: Because our office throws away so much paper

4. **Principal clause:** We stayed in the garden with Dad
   Subordinate clause: since Mum was washing the floors

5. **Principal clause:** Susan has a mobile phone
   Subordinate clause: that she talks on all the time

6. **Principal clause:** He hit a ball directly at me
   Subordinate clause: which I caught

7. **Principal clause:** Mary ate the swordfish at the restaurant
   Subordinate Clause: although she hated it

Page 5
Adjectival Clauses

1. Mike, **whose ancestors came from Ireland**, marched in the St Patrick Day Parade.   Circle—Mike

2. Maths, **which is David's favourite subject**, has always been easy for him. Circle—Maths

3. There is the house **that I'd like to buy.** Circle—house

4. We live an hour from Tullamarine, **which is Victoria's largest airport.** Circle—Tullamarine

5. Is that the jacket **you want to buy?** Circle—jacket

6. Caulfield is the town **where your father was born.** Circle—town

7. Mr Harman is a history teacher **who also coaches basketball.** Circle—teacher

8. Is this the letter **you were expecting?** Circle—letter

9. Across the road is the school **that I attended.** Circle—school

10. For dinner we had fried chicken **which is my favourite dish.** Circle—chicken

Adjectival Phrases

1. I saw an elephant **with a white skin.** Circle—elephant

2. My grandfather is a man **of great wisdom.** Circle—man

3. The price **of the boots** was too high. Circle—price

Page 7
Comprehension

A. Answer the questions

1. The main powers in the struggle were France and England.

2. a. Louis XIV, of France was trying to extend his country's boundaries to the River Rhine.
   b. France was attempting to control the policy of Spain which, if achieved, would have threatened the independence of other European countries.
   c. There was commercial and colonial rivalry between the two countries.

3. It mattered to Louis XIV who ruled on the English throne because if William was successful then he would support Holland and make it impossible for Louis XIV to gain the Netherlands.

4. By 1697 Britain had gained supremacy on the seas.

Australian Homeschooling #563
Successful English 8B

Answers Successful English 8B

5. The question of the Spanish succession was important because of the large territories Spain owned.

6. Britain fought the 1702-1713 war against Spain because they wanted to check France's power; safeguard their trade and prevent the restoration of the Stuart kings.

7. This was the period in history leading up to and just after the settlement of Australia so events then influenced the decision to start colonies in Australia.

B. Vocabulary

1. succession

2. colony

Page 9
Answer the question

1. In both poems the first and third line and the second and fourth line rhyme. (quatrain)

Page 10

2. Answers may vary: The rhymes and short lines help to make the poem flow freely.

3. Answers may vary. Suggestions: A chorus is by necessity repeated several times throughout a ballad, allowing the audience to memorise it and join in.

4. Answers may vary. Suggestions: the poems were easy to remember; they appealed to a population of convicts, all of whom liked to pretend, like prisoners today, that they were innocent; they appealed to prisoners who had feelings of nostalgia for England and who probably remembered their life of freedom there being better than it was.

5. Poems are recited whereas ballads are usually sung.

6. a. shackles or chains, probably with a ball on the end.
   b. wings
   c. Court in London where the prisoner was sentenced.

7. The person who wrote the first ballad appears to be more literate than the person in the second ballad.

8. Van Diemen's Land is now called Tasmania.

9. Botany Bay is in New South Wales.

Page 11
Correct usage

A. Correct verb

1. To every argument there are at least two sides.

2. None of them seem to have made up his mind.

3. A party with a dog team was approaching the outpost.

4. Six weeks' leave per year has been granted to all workers.

5. Each man and woman in the group was carrying a heavy load.

B. Correct Sentences

1. The teacher read "Treasure Island" to them.

2. To both Jane and I the news came as a complete surprise.

3. But I am not the person for whom you are searching.

4. Who do you think has committed the robbery?

5. Paul said he and I were the best players on the team.

Page 12

A. Adjectival Phrase

1. of that city

2. without any children

3. near the door

4. on the deck

5. with good instincts   (a man with) a great sense of humour

6. while walking the dog

B. Adjectival Clause

1. that you brought

2. you asked for

3.   who helped me

© Valerie Marett
Coroneos Publications

Australian Homeschooling #563
Successful English 8B

5. you'd like to buy

6. that you found roaming

7. which is my favourite meal

Page 13
Adjectival clause or phrase

1. who follow the party line
   adjectival clause

2. hearing a step
   adjectival phrase

3. which were not convincing
   adjectival clause

4. when the storm was over
   adjectival clause

5. whom you will not have read
   adjectival clause

6. because of his fine record
   adjectival phrase

7. during her senior year of university
   adjectival phrase

8. that have diesel engines
   adjectival clause

9. that you recommended
   adjectival clause

10. of a Norwegian immigrant
    adjectival phrase

11. with the pleasant smile
    adjectival phrase

12. who was asking for you
    adjectival clause

13. with three children
    adjectival phrase

Page 15
A. Answer the questions

1. Spain had enormous trade possessions in South America.

2. The British had one ship that docked in a port and unloaded by day only to be restocked by small ships under the cover of darkness. They were then able to unload again the following day.

3. France and Britain were rivals in North America. They were seeking to gain land and influence there by establishing colonies.

4. The French started building a long line of fortresses between their southern and northern possessions. The final result of this action was war between the British and French.

5. Building a fort at the junction of three rivers meant that the French controlled all trade, especially the fur trade, that came down these rivers.

B. Word knowledge

1. skirmishes

2. acute

3. incensed

4. disastrous

Page 18
A. Answer the questions

1. Both poems are written as narratives.

2. The common theme of each poem is the adventures of a particular bushranger and the pursuit of the bushrangers by the law.

3. Each poem is divided into stanzas. In "The Wild Colonial Boy" the stanzas are broken up with a chorus.

Page 19

4. "The Wild Colonial Boy" is written in couplets but "The Ballad of Ben Hall" does not rhyme.

5. "We scorn to live in slavery bowed down with iron chains" is the line that would have appealed. Suggestion: There was a strong feeling against the police who were often corrupt as the majority of the population had flocked to the gold fields.

Page 20
Adverbial clauses

1. whenever you are in Werribee
   when—time

2. planting her hands on her hips.
   how—manner

3. since I am late for dinner
   why—reason

   before I return home
   when—time

4. than Joel can (swim)
   how—manner

5. as the rain poured down her back
   when—time

6. as she unpegged her wet washing
   why—reason
   from the line is an adverbial phrase

7. where he had prepared the ground
   where—place

8. as we entered St Vincent's Gulf
   where—place

9. when she heard Krystal scream
   when—time

Page 21
A. Adverbial phrases

1. After school   when

2. for his key   why

3. all day   when

4. at the shops   where

5. in the car   where

6. through the grass   where
   on his belly   how

7. down the dirt road   where

8. to avoid the traffic why

B. Replace phrase with adverb
(Parents to correct. Suggestions below.)

1. without a second's hesitation
   Instantly

2. on the day after today
   tomorrow

3. in the end
   eventually

4. at the correct time
   promptly

Page 23

A. Answer the questions:

1. There was a struggle after the death of the last great Moghul as both countries wanted to gain the greatest commercial advantage by influencing the native rulers.

2. The constant fighting between the native rulers gave the French and British the chance to interfere in India.

3. The French trained Indian forces and began negotiating with native princes to exclude the British from trade.

4. France had gained most of the Carnatic and besieged Madras.

5. Robert Clive seized the native capital of Arcot, drawing off besiegers from Trichnopoly. Then he gradually overran the Carnatic.

6. The naval superiority of the British allowed them to move swiftly to and from India.
   The approval by the British Government of the policies and programmes of the British Company and the lack of French Government interest.
   Their strong financial position.

B. Word Knowledge

1. prestige

2. intriguing

3. besiege

Page 24

A.   Using a Single Word

1. The oil company decided to consult a geologist.

2. Leonardo da Vinci was know for his versatility.

3. He spoke monotonously.

4. A precedent has been developed.

5. Joseph's plans were nebulous. (or uncertain.)

6. I was commended for my resourcefulness.

B. Using disc- words

2. discriminate

3. disclose

4. discord

5. discourteous

6. discipline

7. discus

8. discern

9. discomfort

Page 25

A. -al and –ar

1. consular
2. elemental
3. titular
4. universal
5. familial
6. glandular
7. monumental
8. official

B. Collective nouns

1. chain
2. troupe
3. choir
4. gaggle
5. board
6. school or shoal
7. herd
8. pod
9. pride
10. culture
11. galaxy
12. fleet
13. gang
14. congregation

C. Plurals

1. mosquitoes
2. alleys
3. man-eaters
4. sister-in-laws
5. fishes
6. volcanoes
7. stories
8. flies

9. mercies
10. allies
11. vertices
12. parentheses
13. quizzes
14. cacti

D. Correct Word

1. affect
2. momentous

Page 27—Poetry

A. Answer the questions:

1. The main idea is that life for the squatter on the land is not easy.

2. The poet has used short lines and rapidly changing scenery to give the idea of time passing. The rhythm is quick paced. As you read through the poem you can see that the situation changes rapidly from good to bad and back again.

Page 28

3. couplets

4. The tone of the poem is humorous. The squatter takes both the good and the bad "in his stride." He is a typical farmer.

Page 29

1. The theme of the poem is the love of the farm hand for the free selector's daughter.

2. While both poems are humorous, "The Squatter's Diary" gives us a look at the life of a squatter, whereas "The Free Selector's Daughter" is a light hearted love poem. "The Squatter's Diary covers a much longer period of time than "The Free Selector's Daughter."

3. It refers to the Lachlan River side of the Murray, that is in New South Wales.

4. Answers will vary

Page 30
A. Correct sentence

1. It is one of those books that holds your interest throughout. (or all the way through.) (one requires singular verb)

2. No-one who has his feet on the ground will ever take himself too seriously.

3. To every argument there are at least two sides.

4. Four weeks' leave has been granted to all workers.

5. We weren't surprised at the plan, but now we are faced with the task of preparing a new plan.

6. Each of the men has been told to prepare for a long journey.

7. I am not the person for whom you are searching. (Do not start a sentence with but. Do not end a sentence with a preposition.)

8. It was me who saw you near the gate in the lane.

9. A rise in prices and wages usually go together.

10. Neither he nor I was able to throw any light on the matter.

11. The committee has reached its decision.

12. Both you and I are invited to the party.

Page 31
Proverbs

a. Every cloud has a silver lining

b. Jack of all trades, master of none.

c. Whilst there's life, there's hope.

d. There's many a slip 'twix the cup and the lip.

e. Empty vessels make the most noise.

f. Civility costs nothing.

g. He who pays the piper calls the tune.

h. Nothing ventured, nothing gained.

Page 32
A. Adverbial Clause

1. next to the stream that bubbled over stones
   where—place

2. because he trained so hard
   why—reason

3. when we reached the spring
   when—time

4. as the trainer always tells you
   how—manner

5. as he peered at the map (manner)

B. Adverbial Phrase

1. in the middle of the path
   where—place

2. for medical reasons
   why—reason

3. early in the morning
   when—time

4. in about half an hour
   when—time
   in a taxi
   how—manner

5. on the path
   where—place

Page 33
C. Adverbial phrase or clause

1. because I was very tired
   adverbial clause

2. if we do not hurry
   adverbial clause

3. over the line
   adverbial phrase

4. after I've eaten
   adverbial clause

5. below the sea
   adverbial phrase

6. if you do not hurry
   adverbial clause

D. Adverbial or adjectival clause

1. while the family were on holiday
   adverbial clause

2. which you are visiting
   adjectival clause

3. so that I can still see you
   adjectival clause

Answers Successful English 8B

4. for whom you baked a cake
   (adverbial clause)

5. until the sun set
   adverbial clause

6. as Peter's (house) is
   adverbial clause

Page 35
A. Answer these questions

1. **First Estate:** clergy and the church who had the right to levy a 10% tax
   The Second Estate: nobility, including all the royal family except the king. They paid no tax.
   Third Estate: tradesmen, farmers and peasants who paid tax.

2. The Divine Right of Kings is the belief that the monarch is given the right to rule by God and is subject to no earthly authority.

3. The biggest complaint of the Third Estate was likely to have been that they were the only ones bearing the burden of taxation. They were not only paying tax to the king and nobility but also to the Church.

4. This discontent showed itself firstly in the setting up of a National Assembly and then later, when this was not acknowledged by the King, the storming of the Bastille.

5. No it did not stop. Mobs are not easily controlled. A National Guard was set up on 15th July, 1789 to control the situation.

6. It seems likely he was not guillotined because he was a hero of the American War of Independence.

B. Word Knowledge

1. Estate

2. mob

Page 37
Answer the questions

1. Drought caused Andy to leave, probably both in New South Wales and Queensland.

2. Andy lived in New South Wales. We

know this because he crossed the Darling River, which is in New South Wales, to go to Port Macquarie, also in NSW.

3. He wishes for this because it will bring Andy home.

4. The whole family is feeling the loss of Andy; the selection is dull and seems to lack life; there is no-one to stop the squatter trying to get them to leave; the dog is constantly looking for Andy and howls at night; the gates need fixing and the writer's Aunty and Uncle miss him.

5. The poem is written in four line stanzas with the second and fourth line rhyming.

6. The selector's daughter is probably the person speaking although it could be Andy's mother, the selector's wife. The person speaking is obviously a woman and either daughter or mother of the selector as the poem refers to the squatter trying to get them to leave.

Page 38
Answer the questions:

1. a. **coolibah:** North Australian gum tree which typically grows near watercourses and yields very strong, hard timber.

Page 39

   b. **bronzewing:** an Australian pigeon with a metallic bronze band on its wings

   c. **saplings:** young trees with slender trunks.

   d. **pannikins:** small metal drinking cups

2. The stockman mentions the scrub so we can infer he is in a dry area of the outback. We also know this because there are dingoes in the area. Another reason we know that it is the outback is that the stockman is going to be buried here and not in a cemetery.

3. Each verse is made up of four lines. The second and fourth line of each verse rhymes. There is a chorus in between each verse.

© Valerie Marett
Coroneos Publications

Australian Homeschooling #563
Successful English 8B

Answers Successful English 8B

4. Ballads were often sung around campfires and at get togethers. A catchy tune made it easier for people to remember and sing along to. "The Dying Stockman" is a sad topic but a catchy tune lifts the tone.

Page 40
Answer the questions:

1 a. The summer grass was the colour of the sun.

   b. The coolabah's branches were twisted and were the colour of steel.

2. Time has been personified. In the line "Time waited for the three." Time is made to seem like a person standing still and waiting for the stockman, his horse and his dog. In the line "Time took up his solar swag." Time is made to appear like a person picking up a swag and moving on again.

3. The cattle dog was standing panting with his tongue out.

4. A mirage is an optical illusion caused by atmospheric conditions, especially the appearance of a sheet of water in a desert or on a hot road caused by the refraction of light from the sky by heated air.

5. The mirage distorted the view so the stockman appeared to become younger and the poet could almost believe he was seeing the stockman's grandson. This fits in with the idea of Time distorting so several generations can be seen at once.

6. The second and fourth line of each verse rhymes and so does the fifth and sixth.

7. Answers will vary. Suggestions: It probably was a hot day. Reasons: stockman stopped in the shade, dog is panting, there is a mirage on the plain, the poet refers to "distorting air."

Page 41
Malapropism

1. prodigy   sonatas

2. emphatic

3. amphibious

4. credible

5. monogamy

6. equivocal

7. invention

8. insecticide

9. optimistic

10. masticate

11. debut

Page 42

A. Clauses or Phrases?
Remember: a clause has a subject and a verb. A phrase does not.

1. phrase

2. clause

3. clause

4. phrase

5. clause

6. phrase

B. Subordinate Clause

1. since we expected crowds

2. if you like penguins

3. that carried the sick man

4. since she had seen the movie twice

5. as he waited

6. if you come to my house

Page 43
Sentences

A. Add commas

1. My ice-cream, which is chocolate flavoured, is melting fast.

2. Although I don't want to get sunburnt, I like laying outside on the grass.

3. "I would like to invite you to my party," my friend Veronica said.

4. I bought new shorts, sunglasses, a swimsuit and tank tops for a holiday at the beach.

B. Complex Sentence

1. The highschool band gave an hour long concert.

2. We waited for Frank, David and Peter.

3. When you draw a clown, be sure to give him a funny nose, huge eyes and a big mouth.

4. Mum went to speak to our neighbour who lives across the street.

5. When we reached the stream we drank thirstily.

6. Mr Dexter is my piano teacher of three years.

Page 45
Comprehension

A. Word Knowledge

1. unicameral
2. inalienable
3. schism
4. tithes
5. franchise

B. Answer these questions:

1. The Declaration of the Rights of Man was published. It was published on August 26th, 1789.

2. In Australia colonies in the same period had been started at Sydney Cove and Launceston and were struggling.

3. It was modelled on the Declaration of Independence.

4. The Declaration of Independence protected the rights of the individual whereas the Declaration of the Rights of Man gave the majority in society rights over the individual. (This is democracy.)

5. The Catholic Church at first lost their right to collect money and then, just over a year later, had all their money taken away from them.

Page 46
Poetry
Answer these questions:

1. The ballad is written in a four line verse with a chorus in between each verse. The lines rhyme in couplets.

Page 47

2. Definitions:
   a. ringer

b. bare-bellied joe
c. tar boy
d. swag
e. boss of the board
f. old snagger

3. The poem has a happy tone with a swift rhythm. It epitomizes the Australian love of the underdog, in this case the old shearer.

Page 48

Answer the questions:

1. "Matilda" was the swag carried over his shoulder. It would have contained his bedding, his few possessions and his food.

2. "Matilda" is described as "waltzing." The author is describing the regular movement of the swag as it swung up and down as the swagman walked.

3. a. sheep

   b. a branch of a river, formed by a flood, cut off afterwards and becoming a stagnant pool.

   c. a separate bag containing the swagman's food.

4. If caught by the police the swagman would be imprisoned and the thought of this was unbearable to a person who was used to roaming at will from place to place.

5. Answers will vary. Suggestion: Australia's first settlement was as a convict prison. Many Irish rebels were also sent to or emigrated to Australia. When settlers arrived later they were mostly poor. Both the convicts and the settlers therefore felt more kinship with the under-dog than the Government or the wealthy squatters.

6. Answers will vary

Page 49
Malaproprisms

1. The kennel owner was highly elated when his dog won first prize.

2. Since time immemorial men have striven to better their situation.

3. A lot of people were guillotined during the French Revolution.

4. Keep the rope taut or the tent will fall.

5. He lost marks because much of the material in his essay was irrelevant.

6. He was a boarder at school for five years.

7. The speaker told the students he could not too strongly exhort them to deal with others in a sportsmanlike manner.

8. The coach said he was averse to making any changes in the team.

9. It is beyond my comprehension how you can believe that.

10. I resent that remark. It is just not true!

11. I am inured to my husband's jokes.

12. He exhorted the boy to do his best.

Page 50

Noun clause

1. what my brother enjoys most

2. why she couldn't come to the party

3. whoever was late

4. whoever wins the race

5. what I wonder

Page 51

A. Noun clause and purpose

1. that he would not go
   object of the verb

2. what he says
   object of the preposition "on"

3. that we will have to admit defeat
   in apposition to the pronoun

4. that he is not interested in the offer
   subject of the verb

5. that he was not feeling well
   object of the verb.

6. that he is alive
   in apposition to the noun news

7. where he has gone
   object of the verb know

8. that he was present
   in apposition to the pronoun it

B. Change to a Noun Clause
   (may vary slightly)

2. I don't remember when Mother's Day is.

3. Do you know whose car this is?

4. He would like to know what time the flight arrived.

5. Her mother didn't understand why she couldn't catch the bus on time.

Page 53

A. Answer the question

1. Answers may vary. Suggestions.
   The social order of society had been disrupted.
   People could be executed for little cause.
   The peasants and workers caused unrest, often rioting.

2. Leopold II of Austria refused to return them and called on Europe to help restore Louis XVI to the throne.
   France declared war on Austria. Austria and its allies marched into France capturing towns as they went. They were stopped on the outskirts of Paris by the French artillery followed by the French infantry. The Alliance retreated back to Austria.

3. No it didn't work well. Groups developed within the Assembly and none of the groups were prepared to compromise. Also there was constant fear of the Parisian mob (peasants) who often rioted.

4. Louis was used by a group to manoeuvre one of the opposing groups into a position where they could win over them.

B. Word Knowledge

1. radical

2. compromise

3. balance of power

4. constitutional monarchy

5. agitating

C. Grammar

a Legislative Assembly — subject
had been formed by 1792 —predicate

Page 56

Answer these questions:

1. Eldorado was a mythical, lost city of gold waiting for someone to find it. Whoever found it would have unimaginable riches. Henry Lawson's use of this word suggests

that those who come to the gold fields were expecting to find great wealth.

2. Lawson uses the words "human stream" to describe the people coming. It brings to mind images of water flowing steadily onwards in a given direction.

3. a. The Royal Mail was the most trusted carrier in the United Kingdom so the use of the term implies that the mail was being carried by a trusted company.

   b. Cobb & Co. was a coachline, the principle means of transport in Queensland, New South Wales and Victoria at this time.

Page 57

4. Henry Lawson has personified "Adventure" and (Dame) "Fortune." "Old Adventure" has been personified to give you a better image of what the camp looks like at night. "Dame Fortune" helps the reader understand that whether the digger found gold or not was pure chance.
   Answers will vary.

5. Answers will vary. Make sure the examples are taken from different verses.

6. Answers will vary. Examples: azure line; darkest green; of calico etc. They make the picture he is painting more vivid.

7. These lines are referring to the train line that now unites the city to the bush and runs past the old goldfields.

Page 58

A. Noun Phrase

1. the back door key

2. favourite sports teacher

3. dark horse

4. in time

5. the man guilty

6. by the summer rain

7. about the sports carnival

8. a bank account

B. Noun Phrase or Clause

1. noun clause

2. noun clause

3. noun phrase

4. noun clause

5. noun phrase

Page 59
Choosing better words

1. Our building was in urgent need of renovation.

2. Our team fought tenaciously for victory.

3. Only the most sceptical people were unconvinced.

4. My mother gave me only a cursory glance as I entered the room.

5. Your history essay contains too much extraneous material.

6. Tentative arrangements had been made for the Scout camp.

7. A giggle arose which the teacher quelled with a glance.

8. The debater's fallacious arguments did not deceive the adjudicator.

9. On account of his position in the community his story was given wide credence.

10. Honesty was one of our Prime Minister's most salient traits.

Page 61
Answer these questions:

1. It was struggling because it was being attacked by European enemy forces from Austria. In addition it had trouble from the British Navy who waited just outside French ports ready to connect with the advancing enemy force. The revolutionary groups within the revolution were disunited and their job was not made easier by the peasants who frequently rioted.

2. The real ruling party was the Committee of Public Safety.

3. The sans-culottes were the peasants and tradesman. They had so much influence as there were so many of them and they were prone to riot when dissatisfied.

4. The most positive results were that the Committee agreed to tackle the shortages of food and started to organize the revolutionary armies.

5. Bocquier's Law provided a system of free education for 6-13 year olds. It made homeless children the state's responsibility and they gave inheritance rights to illegitimate children. It further introduced a uniform system of measures and weights.

6. Symbols of Catholicism were smashed, buildings were vandalised and vestments were burnt. To counter the Biblical idea of seven days in a week they introduced a calendar with 10 days in a week, 30 days in a month and 12 months in a year.

B. Word Knowledge

1. albeit

2. federalism

3. tyranny

Page 64

Answer these questions:

1. Yes, the writer is biased. He has written the poem solely from the point of view of the diggers. He has not taken into account the need for police on the diggings, which were fairly lawless places, nor how these police were to be paid.

2. a. **flower of all nations on earth:** flower refers to the young men in their full strength. This is referring to young men who had come from many countries throughout the world.

Page 65

b. **the mark of the cursed broad arrow:** this refers to the black arrow printed on convicts' trousers.

c. **new-chums:** people newly arrived in Australia who didn't understand the country and its customs.

d. **the blood to his forehead was rising:** he was so excited that his face was going red.

e. **a cause that was won by the battle they lost:** the deaths at Eureka Stockade resulted in a change in the law.

3. Bently was a hotel owner who fearing the unrest on the diggings wrote to the authorities asking for help. The diggers burnt down his hotel.

4. Patterson seems to have favoured the

diggers who struck for their rights. It is obvious in the poem that he did not think much of the troopers who enforced the purchase of licences.

A. Story

Parent to mark.

B. Poetry terms

2. onomatopoeia

3. metaphor

4. pun (dreamers also lie in bed)

Page 67
Condense Sentences

1. We never learn from historical mistakes.

2. The weather is unexpected.

3. He spoke angrily.

4. Everyday he works from first light. (or sunrise)

5. Answer your letters immediately.

6. The old man looked very happy. or The old man was ecstatic.

7. A lawyer dying intestate was strange.

8. He quickly achieved his aim.

9. I know the figures add up. or I know the figures are correct.

Page 69

A. Answer the questions:

1. These years were important because the year he was born Corsica became French and Napoleon therefore had a French education and military training. After his training he returned to Corsica where he became affiliated with the Jacobins. Both of these gave him opportunities for advancement at a later date.

2. Napoleon believed that the French naval force was not yet strong enough to beat the British navy.

3. Napoleon proposed instead to invade Egypt in an effort to wipe out British trade routes with India.

4. At first he appeared to succeed when he won a victory against the Egyptian military rulers at the Battle of the Pyramids. However this was short lived, as his army was stranded after the French Navy

Answers Successful English 8B

was defeated by the British at the Battle of the Nile.

5. Napoleon next turned towards the Ottoman-ruled Syria. No he failed.

6. Napoleon returned to France because he was ambitious and he felt the unrest there gave him an opportunity to become part of a group that overthrew the Directory. Yes, it was a wise decision because he was soon appointed First Consul.

7. centralised government
    instituted reforms in education and government
    supported science and art
    sought to improve relations with the Pope
    Napoleonic Code—streamlined legal system

8. Parent to check

B. Word Knowledge

1. insurrection

2. decimated

3. cemented

4. affiliated

Page 72
Answer the questions

1. Answers will vary. Suggestions:
    Where a horse's hoofs strike firelight
    from the flint stones every stride
    You can visualise the horse being ridden hard over stony (flint) ground.
    And they charged beneath the stockwhip
    with a sharp and sudden dash,
    Conjures up images of a troop of horses charging straight at Clancy to get past him and escape.
    And he raced him down the mountain like
    a torrent down its bed,
    The image is of a raging stream— torrent— which gives the reader an excellent idea of how fast the Man From Snowy River rode down the hill.

Page 73

2. Suggestions: raced away, racing on the wing, fast the horsemen followed, raced him down the mountain, at a racing pace, as he raced across the clearing

in pursuit, wild horses racing yet, their sides were white with foam.

3. Some suggestions:
    Where the river runs those giant hills
    between;
    the big mimosa clump
    the gorges deep and black
    cliffs and crags that beetled overhead
    Where mountain ash and kurrajong
    grew wide
    wild hop scrub grew thickly
    Through the stringybarks and saplings,
    on the rough and broken ground,
    The words paint a vivid picture of the roughness of the country through which the horsemen travelled. Without these word pictures it would be impossible to understand the difficulties the horsemen faced.

4. The poem is written in stanzas with alternate lines rhyming.

5. Answers will vary. Parent to mark. Suggestion: the poet obviously loved the bush and bush stories. The feat by the Man from Snowy River was based on an actual episode and to Patterson it epitomised the best of the bush.

6. Answers will vary. Parent to mark.

Page 74
Types of sentences.

A. Simple Sentences

Parent to mark. A few examples have been given.

2. Into the room was suddenly flung a straw hat.

3. The boy chose the largest cake.

4. Where did you put the set of screwdrivers?

B. Combine as Complex Sentences
Answers may vary. Suggestions. Make sure that the answer is **not** a simple sentence.

1. We prefer wool, which makes the best suits.

2. I was driving along Smith Street when I was hailed by a man. or
    As I was driving along Smith Street I was hailed by a man.

3. It was last year when Mary Jones went to Japan.

Answers Successful English 8B

4. The sheriff, whom you met in the canyon today, shot the bandits.

Page 75
A. Complex sentence by using a conjunction

1. He opened his book **and** read a chapter.

2. Nearly a month has passed **before** (or **since**) I received your email.

3. I can not buy a bicycle **until** I have saved more money.

4. Andrew did not pass his exam **because** he did not study.

5. They arrived **while** I was still eating my breakfast.

B. Add phrase or clause.
Answers will vary. A few examples have been given below to help.

1. I would have never believed that I could get the job finished so quickly.

2. Standing on his toes he could just see over the top.

3. He asked if anyone would mind if he opened the window.

4. I have never quite understood why pictures have replaced words on many signs.

5. Thought I tried very hard I will never be able to draw very well.

6. The tractor, that I had borrowed from Jack, broke down on the way to the paddock.

7. Yesterday morning I discovered a tennis ball hidden in the long grass.

Page 77
A. Word Knowledge

1 divert

2. amphibious

3. seceded

4. solidifying

5. eliminated

B. Answer these questions

1. Napoleon was planning to attack England. If he had landed his army the English would have been defeated because while they were supreme at sea they did not have a strong enough army to defend England.

2. Napoleon was diverted by the Russian and Austrian army attacking France.

3. Napoleon's fleet was defeated at the Battle of Trafalgar on October 21st, 1805.

4. Napoleon defeated Russia, Austria and Prussia.

5. Napoleon decided instead to try and defeat England economically. To do so he tried to restrict England from trading with Europe by demanding his Empire close their ports to the English.

6. England, in return, created a blockade of European ships anywhere on the ocean they had control.

C. Battle of Trafalgar
Parent to mark.

Page 79
Answer the questions:

1. The poem is written with alternate lines rhyming.

2. The poem's theme is the platypus and it contains a description of what he looks like and where he lives.

3. Answers may vary. Suggestions: Paterson has used words like "sweep and shiver" to describe the movement of the reeds. He has used the words "drifting down," "plays and dives," and "sank" to describe the movements of the platypus in the river.

4. Answers may vary. Suggestions: Paterson describes the platypus as being "velvety brown" which leaves the reader with the image of the platypus's smooth coat. His burrow is described as being below a bank with an under water entrance. Apart from his family his life is solitary. He finishes by describing how different the platypus is.

5. Parents to mark. Answers will vary.

Page 80

1. The theme is the vastness and beauty of the Gulf area he is describing and the smallness of man when compared to it.

Answers Successful English 8B

2. Answers may vary. Parent to mark. Some examples: a great grey chaos; sphinx-like visage; languid motion; mighty plain and river.

3. Nature has been personified as an old woman.
   Answers will vary. Parent mark.

Page 81

4. Man is described as being weak and powerless as an insect compared to the vastness of the plains and rivers. He is also described as having a life that lasts only a moment compared to the time-lessness of the land.

5. Answers will vary. Parents to mark.

Correct Word

1. aquatic
2. irascible
3. rotary
4. vindictive
5. contemptuous
6. ponderous
7. auxiliary
8. pensive

Page 82
Word Meanings

1. profile
2. garrulous
3. parapet
4. calamity
5. biennial
6. avaricious
7. lament
8. militant
9. complacent
10. symptom
11. enumerate
12. infectious
13. consequence
14. monotonous
15. inaudible
16. obscure
17. intangible
18. scrupulous

Page 83
A. Add adverbial phrase or clause.

Remember a phrase does not contain a verb. A clause can stand alone, so see if the ending, provided by the child, does this.

Parent to mark. **A couple of examples are given to help you**.

1. After dinner I will wash the dog.

3. This week he is bowling better than he bowled last week.

4. In spite of the heat we enjoyed ourselves immensely.

B. Add a clause.
Parent to mark. A couple of examples are given.

1. The child who crosses the road without looking is likely to get run over.

2. An instrument, which magnifies very small objects, is called a microscope.

Page 85
A. Answer the questions:

1. Under the Continental System most of Europe was intended to trade between themselves and refuse to trade with Britain, starving their manufacturing industries of both the raw material and trade they needed.

2. No, it did not achieve its aim. The English simply traded with their colonies. The internal European economy was slowed by the System as all trading products had to be sent by land. In addition France imposed a tariff on products coming into France, but no tariff was imposed on products leaving France. It also led to the Peninsula War that sapped French strength.

3. The Empire included France, Belgium, Holland, parts of Germany and the Italian coast up to Rome. Alliances were held with Austria, Russia, Denmark, Sweden and Prussia.

4. Through his dominance of Europe Napoleon spread the Napoleonic Code, with minor changes, to all of his territories. He

© Valerie Marett
Coroneos Publications

Australian Homeschooling #563
Successful English 8B

did what he could to end feudal peasantry and make all citizens are equal before the law.

5. Napoleon saw his Empire as a recreation of the Roman Empire.

6. Australia sent her first shipment of wool to England in 1811. The wool industry developed into a thriving industry.

B. Word Knowledge

1. morale

2. crucial

3. code

C. Research and Write could to end feudal peasantry.

Answers will vary. Parents to mark. Some things to investigate: mechanisation of factories, especially cotton and woollen mills; changes in farming.

Page 87
Answer these questions:

1. The country she is referring to is Australia.

2. The country referred to in the first verse is England.

3. Answers will vary. Any of the following:
—droughts and flooding rains
—stark white ring-barked forests (and) sapphire misted mountains
—flood and fire and famine
—wilful, lavish land

4. Answers will vary. Suggestion: England, mentioned in the first verse she has described in softer tones. Australia, in the second verse is described using more vivid colours, e.g., sunburnt (red-brown) and expressions.

5. a. onomatopoeia: drumming of an army. (creates a feel of soldiers that are marching to the beat of nature.)

   b. personification: the use of "she" and "her". This makes the reader feel Australia is not just a lifeless piece of land.

Page 88

   c. alliteration: "lithe lianas," "flood and fire and famine." The use of alliteration helps to illustrate the characteristics of

Australian rural life.

6. answers will vary. Suggestions: far horizons, jewel seas, rugged mountains, pitiless blue skies.

7. Answers will vary. Parents to mark.

Page 89
Answer these questions:

1. Answers will vary: Some suggestions: grassy knolls, forest heights, myrtle and rose, hill and plain, dark unfathomed mine, childish glee mingling with nature's hidden minstrelsy, mountain top to girdling sea.

2. a. azure bright: bright blue

   b. quaffed: drunk up

   c. mammon: the world—the mine provides gold for those who are more interested in wordly things than nature.

3. Answers will vary. Suggestions: "My Country" is a more realistic description of Australia, whereas "The Song of Australia" is more idealistic.

Page 90

4. floating free   banner bear

5. The repetition has the effect of bringing the reader back to the topic of the poem.

6. The tone of the poem is feverishly patriotic. It is obvious the author is proud of her country.

Indirect Speech

1. Dismayed, Mrs Brown said that she had broken another glass.

2. Father told his small son that he should put the vase down at once.

3. Stella said the stars were brilliant tonight.

4. Robert exclaimed that it was a nice morning and then asked how Tony he was doing.

5. The guard snappily ordered them out straight away.

6. Margaret begged her Mother to buy her one.

7. James said that he really liked their

music and thought it the best song they had ever sung.

Page 91
Colon

1. I wish I had a job: I'm a great worker and I need the money.

2. I have three objections to the plan: it would take too long, cost too much and be too dangerous.

3. The friends I play with are: Jill, Jack, Tom and Eden.

4. Wayne excels in the following sports: cricket, basketball and rowing.

5. My alarm clock is set for 6:45 a.m.

6. You will need the following back to school items: pencils, erasers and markers.

Page 93
A. Word Knowledge

1. confronted
2. retaliating
3. incensed
4. abdicated
5. utilised

B. Answer the questions

1. Napoleon invaded Russia because Russia withdrew from the Continental System and began trading openly with England.

2. Rather than fighting Napoleon, the Russians retreated, burning the country behind them. Napoleon generally didn't supply his army but allowed it to live off the land it captured so the French Army was soon starving.

3. Napoleon's army was also handicapped by a harsh Russian winter that came early and a lack of accommodation and warmth for the men.

4. Napoleon raised another army but this army was not as well trained as those who had died. This aided his defeat.

5. Napoleon abdicated on April 4th, 1814. He was replaced by Louis XVIII.

6. European Common Market or European Union.

Page 94
Answer the questions:

1. Answers may vary slightly. These pioneers were daring. They chopped down trees and ploughed and sowed the land. They were not afraid to live roughly. They worked tirelessly. They created cities and towns people now live in.

Page 95

2. The poet hopes that the present generation will look after what has been produced by the hard work of the pioneers.

3. The poet has used contrasts to suggest passing time. He contrasts the hard work the pioneers did with the fact that now they are old, "snow in our hair," and they are bent. He also contrasts the hueing out of land and tracks within the bush to the noisy cities full of shops, trains and smoke.

4. The effect is created by the short lines, rhyming in the second and fourth lines and finally the short verses.

Answer the questions:

1. The Southern Cross is the other constellation mentioned. (The stars appear to become lower near to dawn.)

Page 96

2. Answers will vary. Suggestions: "shadowy reaches……. purple blackness ……. grey awakening….. heralded the light." These words help the reader to imagine the darkness fading into light.
"pearly dew of the dawning…...sun came up from the ocean, red with cold sea mist." This furthers the idea of a rising sun.

3. By making the last words in each couplet rhyme the poet has enhanced the picture he is presenting. Sometimes the words complement each other, e.g., "sea….free" and in other cases they contrast, e.g., "night….light."

4. Answers will vary. Suggestions: "the shining tree tops kissed" "dying darkness"—this may also be considered personification.

Answers Successful English 8B

5. Answers will vary. Parent to mark.

Page 97
Answer these questions:

1. Answers will vary. Suggestions:
   harsh land..... ring music
   heat to mist
   spring flowers and dead grass

2. The poet loves Australia in all of its moods.

3. Answers will vary. Suggestions:
   "hides the summer rain in a mud-red shirt" —-the rain turns the red dirt to mud that covers the whole land in the same way a shirt covers a body.
   "spring flowers and dead grass"—the grass flowers in spring and then dries in the heat of summer.
   "dead grass, straw to my bricks"—straw used to be incorporated into the mud to give strength when bricks were made. The poet is perhaps suggesting that the contrast of the land adds strength to his writing.

4. The form is not uniform. The first three verses are of similar length but the fourth verse has a longer last line, even though there are still three lines. After the fourth verse the number of lines in a verse varies. This pattern strengthens the contrasts in the land the poet describes.

5. Answers will vary. Parents to mark.

Page 98
Word Meanings

1. digression
2. pursue
3. precis
4. melancholy
5. contemporary
6. repetition
7. prejudice
8. villainous
9. sufficient
10. unanimous

Change to Adjectives
1. comical
2. conclusive
3. contradictable
4. ridiculous
5. acquiescent
6. adversarial

7. absent
8. humble
9. deceptive
10. resentful

Change to Verbs
1. reconcile
2. excel
3. hinder
4. humiliate

Page 99
Anachronisms

1. Cleopatra travelled down the Nile in a beautifully decorated boat (barge.)

2. The quill pen, with which John signed the Magna Carta, is now in the British Museum.

3. The First World War came to an end in 1918 when the Germans were forced to seek an armistice.

4. Julius Caesar was stabbed to death near the Theatre of Pompey.

5. In 1851 Hargraves found specks of gold in Summer Hill Creek.

6. Napoleon's troops were smashed by British soldiers at Waterloo.

7. The French aided American troops in the War of Independence.

8. Shakespeare based one of his plays on English history. (e.g., Henry V.)

Page 100
Noun Clause

1. the mess they made in the hall
   object (of a preposition)

2. what you said
   (direct) object

3. whoever first travelled by sea
   subject

4. whoever wins the race
   object (indirect)

5. that Margaret would leave early
   predicate

6. how the trick was done
   object (of preposition)

7. what I ordered
   predicate

8. what to do next
(direct) object

9. whatever you choose
subject

10. why she couldn't come to the party
(direct) object

11. What my brother enjoys most
subject

12. why the flight was delayed
(direct) object

Page 101
Adverbial Clauses

1. adverbial clause of time
when modifies **arrived**

2. adverbial clause of time and manner
as modifies **look**
when modifies **brewing**

3. adverbial clause of reason
because modifies **was heavy**

4. adverbial clause of condition
if modifies **relaxes**

5. adverbial clause of comparison
than modifies **are** (understood)

Page 103
A. Answer these questions:

1. 26th April, 1564   23rd April, 1616

2. King's New Grammar School

3. Yes. Answers will vary. Suggestion: Education would have made a huge difference to his life. The ability to read and write opened up many more career opportunities in a time when the majority were illiterate. Without this ability to read and write Shakespeare would not have been able to write his many plays and generations would have missed out on the enjoyment of them.

4. Any order. Richard III, A Midsummer Night's Dream, Romeo and Juliet, Merchant of Venice, Julius Caesar, Hamlet, Othello, Macbeth, King Lear.

5. The Globe Theatre is often associated with Shakespeare's plays. It was an outdoor theatre, octagonal in shape and three stories high. It could seat 3,000 people.

B. Essay
Parent to mark.

C. Synonyms
Answers may vary.

1. wealth, affluence   hardship
2. troupe, group
3. building, premises
4. inflexible, rigid   flexible
5. unruly, boisterous   calm, restrained
6. connected, related   unrelated
7. dominance, superiority

Page 104
Define homonyms. Write sentence.
Parents to mark sentences.

1. **aerie:** nest of eagle or other bird of prey
airy: spacious, well ventilated

2. **cereal:** any grass cultivated for the edible parts of its grain
serial: arranged or happening in series

3. **complacent:** satisfied with how things are
complaisant: willing to please

4. **cue:** anything that excites to action; signal
queue: file or line, braid of hair hanging down the back.

5. **file:** a folder for holding paper, a collection of papers
phial: a glass container for holding liquids

6. **leased:** rented
least: minimum

7. **peak:** mountain top
peek: secret look
pique: feeling of resentment arising from a slight

8. **precedence:** priority
precedents: established course of action
presidents: the elected heads of a republic state

Page 105
Noun Equivalents
Answers may differ. Suggestions below.

1. He preferred relying on the generosity of others.

2. I like to read novels and adventure stories.

3. Our captains knows which is the best course to take.

4. Only the just deserve the fair.

5. Who dislikes swimming? or
Who dislikes to swim?

6. Realising the ship was sinking we took to the boats.

7. Depending on the kindness of others for a job was his plan.

8. The well should help the sick.

Page 107
Background to Settlement

A. Word Knowledge

1. fallow

2. phenomenal

3. leguminous

4. scythe

5. nutrients

B. Answer these questions:

1. During the Middle Ages villages had strips of land in various fields and were forced, by necessity, to grow the same type of crops as the other villagers.

2. As a result of the Enclosure Act land was fenced and redistributed. This led to farmers having all of their land together, rather than distributed over several fields. As a result production on farms increased. Farms became larger as wealthy farmers bought up smaller farms and existing farmers became tenant farmers or moved to the towns looking for work.

3. Answers will vary. See text.

4. Students should discuss two of the following: dung pits, better drainage, selective breeding or better transport.

5. Yes, better farming methods helped Britain survive the European Blockade. Better farming methods meant better and larger crops. The increase in corn prices encouraged farmers to produce more crops to sell within Britain.

Page 109
Which category?
1. tragedy
2. romance
3. tragedy
4. history

5. comedy

Page 111
Summary

Parent to check.

Page 112
Hyphens

1. My great-grandfather fought in World War I.

2. Please return the completed form in the self-addressed envelope.

3. Now I am at university I am semi-independent.

Page 113
Brackets

1. Do you like rich food (even if it's bad for you)?

2. The other man (David Johnson) refused to make a statement.

3. He had three interest in his life: (a) his work (b) his children (c) golf.

Dash

1. For tonight's homework, read chapters 16-24.

2. Be sure to bring some warm clothes—among other things a jumper and woollen socks.

Page 115
Answer these questions:

1. Skilled workers arrived from Europe, driven out of their homes by religious persecution.

2. Answers may vary slightly. The whole of the country was powered by coal during the industrial revolution. A great deal of coal was used to produce steel and make machines for use in industry. Most of these machines were powered by water or coal.

3. The cottage industries were generally not the main source of income and were produced as and when the person had time. (For example, weaving cloth.) They were only looking to supplement their income and were not therefore interested in producing huge amounts.

Answers Successful English 8B

4. Production speeded up because England's colonies demanded more and more manufactured goods and were able to supply England with immense quantities of raw material.

5. Britain had large coal fields making coal readily available.
   She had suitable main harbours for shipping goods.
   She was geographically in the centre of the industrial world and had ships to carry goods.
   Labour was readily available due to decreased labour needs on farms.
   Capital was available both from the aristocracy and later from manufacturers who had become wealthy.

B. Word Knowledge

1. immense
2. aristocracy
3. persecution

Page 116
Find the Word

1. adversary
2. turbulent
3. authentic
4. notorious
5. eminent
6. acquiesced
7. allusion
8. intercede
9. hilarious
10. cited
11. ludicrous
12. prolific

Page 117
Synonym

1. initiate   d. commence
2. scheme   f. conspire
3. sombre   g. solemn
4. adept   b. proficient
5. schedule   i. timetable
6. lethal   c. destructive
7. chagrin   e. displeasure
8. deluge   k. inundate
9. pursue   n. chase
10. implore   h. supplicate
11. hoard   l. stockpile
12. lithe   m. supple

13. accede   j. accept
14. ratify   a. confirm

Antonym

1. secluded   d. accessible
2. miser   g. philanthropist
3. transient   a. permanent
4. abundance   e. scarcity
5. immutable   b. changeable
6. abolition   c. establishment

Page 119
Answer the questions:

1. a tragic flaw
   supernatural elements
   internal or external conflict
   fate or fortune
   the theme of foul and revenge
   paradox of life

2. Answers will vary. Parents to check.

Page 120
Comma vs Semicolon

1. The hill was covered with wildflowers; was a beautiful sight.

2. The house was clean, the table set, and the porchlight on; everything was ready for the guests' arrival.

3. As I turned around, I heard a loud thump, for the cat had upset the goldfish bowl.

4. I thought registration day would be tiring, but I didn't know I would have to stand in so many lines.

5. Many companies make sugar-free soft drinks that are flavoured by artificial chemicals; the drinks usually contain only one or two calories per serving.

6. Mr Green, the plumber; George Crompton, the painter; and Bill Stephens were at the party.

or

Mr Green the plumber, George Crompton the painter and Bill Stephens were at the party.

7. The little boy was bright; for example, he could already do division.

© Valerie Marett
Coroneos Publications

Australian Homeschooling #563
Successful English 8B

8. The bus stop, worse luck, was three blocks away; and Jim, thoroughly drenched by the rain, headed for it at a gallop.

9. The dog, growling and snarling, snapped at me; I was so frightened that I ran.

Page 121
Confusing Pairs

1. principal
2. liable
3. ingenious
4. complacent
5. causal
6. cited
7. ceded
8. climactic
9. imminent
10. intolerable
11. monetary
12. proceed
13. collaborated
14. consistently
15. uninterested
16. razed

Page 123
A. Word Knowledge

1. catastrophic
2. atrocious
3. rife
4. nimbler
5. pauper

B. Answer these questions:

1. Answers may vary. Many of the working class had been forced off the farms into the city where they were paid a very small wage. Men were especially disadvantaged as factory and mill owners preferred women and children as they were cheaper. Living conditions were also far worse in the city where three families might be squashed into rooms intended for one family.

2. The areas that most affect health in cities today are sewerage and rubbish collection. Poorer city areas during the Industrial Revolution had neither.

3. The passing of the Factories Act and Mines Act
   growth of democracy and trade unions

4. Answers will vary. Should include: building of canals, improvement in roads and introduction of railways.

5. Answers will vary. Should include: railways were cheaper, faster and could carry more passengers or goods.

Page 124
Find the Word

1. surrender
2. cadaverous
3. didactic
4. palatable
5. beverage
6. etiquette
7. elite
8. extrovert
9. gourmet
10. exorbitant

Clichés

1. d
2. j
3. e
4. a
5. h
6. g
7. c
8. i
9. f
10. b

Page 125
Add a Subject and Main Clause

Answers will vary. Parent to mark.

Compound sentences

1. The trees, mainly varieties of the eucalyptus family, are beautiful native species.

2. My mind was fuzzy and all sorts of funny things seemed to be happening to me; for example, I seemed to be floating, and I felt as light as a feather.

3. I remember very vividly my first attempt at skiing, especially the sprained ankle and the hospital they took me to.

Page 127
Answer these questions:

1. a struggle for lovers to overcome problems

the plot
themes of love and friendship
discord and resolution
hero
number of acts
characters
language
ethical principles

Page 128

2. focus on English monarchs
   not historically accurate
   explores the social structure of the time
   represents the compromise of life

3. Answers will vary. Parents to check.

Word Association

2. epidemic
3. repudiate
4. concussion
5. inhibit
6. optician
7. pneumonia
8. infectious or infection
9. frivolous

Page 131

Answers will vary. Parents to mark.